James E Matthew,
Fre

de

ric Masson

Napoleon at Home

The daily life of the emperor at the Tuileries

James E Matthew,
Fre

de

ric Masson

Napoleon at Home
The daily life of the emperor at the Tuileries

ISBN/EAN: 9783337350499

Printed in Europe, USA, Canada, Australia, Japan

Cover: Foto ©ninafisch / pixelio.de

More available books at **www.hansebooks.com**

Napoleon at Home

*THE DAILY LIFE OF THE EMPEROR
AT THE TUILERIES*

BY

FRÉDÉRIC MASSON

TRANSLATED BY

JAMES E. MATTHEW

WITH TWELVE ILLUSTRATIONS BY F. DE MYRBACH

VOL. I.

LONDON
H. GREVEL AND CO.
PHILADELPHIA: J. B. LIPPINCOTT COMPANY
1894

Printed by Hazell, Watson, & Viney, Ld., London and Aylesbu

CONTENTS OF VOL. I.

	PAGE
INTRODUCTION . .	ix

I. ETIQUETTE . .   1

The old and the new *régime*—The King—The Nobility—The Clergy—The Third Estate—The People—The principle of authority abolished by the Revolution — The necessity Napoleon was under to re-establish it—The origin which he assigns to his power—Charlemagne—Strange resemblance of the situations—Formation of the Court on the example of the Carlovingian Court—Grand dignitaries—Grand officers of the Empire—Grand officers of the Crown—Etiquette—The reason of its existence—By it alone absolute monarchies exist—Bourbon etiquette—Napoleon unable to re-establish it in its entirety—The reason of this inability—The King—The Emperor—The Conciliator—Service of honour—Service of actual necessity—Apartment of honour—Private apartment—The true life of Napoleon goes on in the private apartment.

II. THE APARTMENTS. THEIR PROTECTION   . 53

Where to look for the apartments of the Emperor—The arrangement of them more important than the furniture—

Division of the apartments of the palace—State apartments—Ordinary apartments—Apartment of honour—Interior apartment—Secret apartment—Arrangement of the rooms—Posts of the guard—The *Adjoints* of the palace—Reynaud—Clément—Ségur—Tascher—The Governor of the palace—The Under-Governor—The *adjudant* Auger—The rounds of the guard—Anecdotes—How the Emperor was guarded in the interior apartment—Proposed formation of companies of body-guards at the end of 1812.

III. THE TOILET . . . 74

The Emperor's bedroom—His awakening—The first *valet-de-chambre*, Constant—The admission of a courier—The service of health—Yvan—Corvisart—Tea—The bath—*Valets-de-chambre* of the toilet—Roustam, Saint-Denis, called Ali—Wages and perquisites—The beard—Large use of water—Pedicure—The hair-dresser—The way the Emperor wore his hair—Use of flesh-brush—Dressing—Concealed poison—Stockings—Shoes—Boots—Waistcoat—Sword—*Grand coraon*—Grenadier's coat—Frock of a *chasseur à cheval*—Decorations—The Master of the Wardrobe—Rémusat—Turenne—Hat—Pocket-handkerchief—Eyeglasses—Bonbon-box—Snuff-box—Watches—Money.

IV. THE MORNING LEVÉE . . . 132

The chamberlain of the day—The *salon de service*—The service—The *grand entrées*—The *salon* of the ordinary apartment—The *Lever*—Audiences—Favours granted—Etiquette observed at audiences.

V. Déjeuner 149

Déjeuner waits—Service of *déjeuner*—Guignet, known as Dunan, *maître d'hôtel*—The *menu*—How the Emperor took *déjeuner*—His tastes in cookery—The soldier's soup—A hair—*Crépinettes* of partridge—Chambertin—Table service and plate—The King of Rome at *déjeuner*—Children—Talma—Denon—Fontaine—His companions in Egypt—The kitchens—The *chefs*.

VI. The Emperor's Study 172

Visits to the Empress—The Study—Its furniture—The back cabinet—The topographical cabinet—The private secretary—Meneval—Fain—The keeper of the portfolio—The secretaries of the cabinet: Clarke, Mounier, and the office of translators—Deponthon—The topographical office—Bacler d'Albe—The library—Denina, Ripault, Barbier—Expenses of the Library—Bindings—Books printed by order of the Emperor—Care which he took of books—Writing paper—Lists—Boxes with divisions—Manuscript dictionaries.

INTRODUCTION.

THE portrait of such a man as Napoleon is not painted at the first attempt. One study does not suffice, nor does one canvas. To attempt, after the lapse of almost a century, to represent so difficult a model with at least some appearance of truth, it is necessary to become imbued with his personality under every aspect which it assumes, according to the time of the day and the variation of the light; to neglect none of those methods of procedure which tend to the acquisition of a portion, however slight, of the actual truth: to study each line, to detail each wrinkle, to photograph each surface and each curve of the countenance; and to relax the work only when it has been carried as far as the resources of art and the most scrupulous attention will allow. For the accessories, and for each one of them, the same labour is required; they must be isolated, and the construction of each one separately investigated; they must be dissected, for in each he has probably included something of himself; they must be grouped together, for it is essential that he should be placed in his own surroundings, and move in his own atmosphere. These are the sketches which a painter, careful of the truth, must fill in before approaching his canvas. At a later time, perhaps, he will attempt to combine all these slight and scattered works in order to construct the portrait he dreams of, but for this, conscientiousness and application will not suffice. In vain he will endeavour to combine his studies, yet never will he succeed in representing as he conceived it, illumined by the glory which flashes from it, the sovereign image of him who among men was the nearest approach to that which is called a God. Possibly even he will never attempt it, so weak does he feel his effort, and so unequal to the task his power; but these studies which he has prosecuted with absolute sincerity, he may hope will preserve in the eyes of the public their truth and their characterisation, and that they will at a later time furnish some one more skilful with the features and expression of nature, and it is for this reason, knowing that life is short, that he sends them forth from his studio and exhibits them.

Such is the scope of these volumes. They have no pretension of offering the last word on him about whom history will occupy itself unceasingly; their aim is simply to fix certain guiding-marks, and to bring into prominence certain characteristic facts. Before every attempt at synthesis, it is by a succession of analyses, slow, accurate, and minute, that we must proceed, and these volumes contain, according to the term used in Germany, no more than contributions to history.

In a previous volume I attempted to define the extent and nature, in the case of Napoleon, of his taste and feelings towards woman; how far his senses affected him, how far his feelings might have been modified either by education or by his exercise of supreme power; how he was affected outwardly and inwardly by that strongest of all passions—Love. I shall attempt later to determine how far he was acted on by the hereditary notions of family feeling, the developments he gave to them, and how far he yielded or resisted them; for it is this feeling which, after love, is the least conventional, the one which man holds most directly from nature. Afterwards I shall investigate the treatment he adopted towards his fellow-creatures, women in particular; what lot he assigned to them, what duties he traced out for them, what relations he had with them, apart from love; for woman is the principal bond of all civilised society, and the social being which man is, only becomes intelligible and definite by his relations with women.

Side by side—and this is the aim of another series of investigations, of which I publish here the first instalment—I propose to give a detailed account of the habits and the rule of life which Napoleon laid down for himself, to describe his dwelling with exactness, to follow him about in it for a whole day, from morning to evening, in such a manner that the reader may be able to arrive at clear ideas when he is spoken of, so that he may figure him, if not as he was actually, at least as it is permissible, after a century, to suppose he was. Having thus described the daily round of this existence, it will be necessary later to describe the entertainments and the pleasures which the Emperor gave to his

Court rather than to himself,—the plays, the concerts, the balls; and then to make the retinue of public appearances pass before us, and to display the whole pomp of the ceremonies. It will be necessary, again, to descend to the trifling details of the organisation of the Imperial household, to call to life again the crowd of chamberlains, equerries, masters of the ceremonies, officers of the hunt, and prefects of the palace; to show whence these people come, and whither they go; how they are recruited, what money and what honours they received, and in what way they paid their debt of gratitude. Finally, leaving Paris, it will be necessary to follow the Court in its small and great journeys to Fontainebleau, to Compiègne, to Rambouillet, and then to those distant residences which the Imperial constitutions fixed in different points of the Empire. An account must be given of his habits and his character; his attire and his pleasures must be described, and the ultimate forms which the Imperial monarchy gave to the country trips of a sovereign must be noted.

Such is a part of the work undertaken, that which, at the present time, seems to the author to be so far advanced that it is not being too bold to announce the plan. He disguises neither the difficulties nor the trouble. To clear up each of the points which he studies successively, he should isolate it and examine it through the microscope. From such a course, no doubt, will result a distorted enlargement which may lead the reader to take a part for the whole, and to make up his mind before all the elements of conviction have been put before him. In closely grouping facts which, spread over a whole life, possess but a moderate importance, we lend to them a seriousness and a connection which they do not really possess. Take the chase, for example. It is attempted in a book to give an account solely of Napoleon as a sportsman; the author must enter into the details of the organisation of the chase; he must have collected the most trifling incidents of each run, have related from the detailed account each whoop; he must follow the Emperor in his shooting parties, setting down the list of each, with the names of the guests and the number of guns. That would be the subject undertaken, and it would be his duty to exhaust it. But when he came to the end of the volume the reader might run away with the notion that during all his life Napoleon did nothing else than hunt, at the very time when he was probably occupied with something quite different.

Here lies the danger of these monographs. Taken by themselves, they give only a moderately exact idea of the model, although, alone, each of the alleged facts may be authentic. In bringing them together, possibly, the outlines will be recovered, and the accumulation of details will give less shadow to the figure. But beyond this what system can be adopted which allows of the acquisition of precise notions, and which does not offer more serious evils?

To understand Napoleon at the present time it will not suffice to give an example of style written in a lazy manner at the corner of a table. Truly his life offers rare material for poetic development. Granted. But the generation which preceded ours excelled in that art, and, from Byron to Hugo, has left scarcely any themes to treat. The cycle is not yet shut; in our days, young men with rolling words and violent images undertake to translate the immortal epic; but however excited their prose may be, the ideas of which they make use, and even their imagery, cannot possibly be new. They transcribe, in the language of to-day and to-morrow, the songs, incorrect and old in form, which for half a century have consoled the Nation, and have kept him before her eyes; which, during the worst ages she has had to pass through, have sustained her pride in herself, the rhythms of which at the present day seem worn out only because they have drawled out so long from the throat of the people. Will the songs of the present day possess this same glory, and awaken the same echoes? No one wishes this more than I; but singing is the business of the young, and because Legend ought to maintain its rights over the soul of France, will it be asserted that History ought to abandon its own rights?

Well then, one will help forward the other: the inquiry which History will set on foot will in no respect tend to destroy Legend; for Legend is but historic truth,—turned into poetry if you will, added to and generalised in certain directions, but almost always strangely exact. History will bring to light new elements of which to-morrow Legend will make use, which it will raise to sublimity at its will, the outlines of which it will soften off and shade, lending it that lofty spirit of poetry with which the imagination alone of the people can surround its hero.

But what is wanted is a history, clear, accurate, based entirely on documents which are trustworthy; a history which goes down to the minutest detail, which leaves no ears of corn to glean on the field which it has chosen for itself. A history is wanted written with no other object in view than the search after truth, apart from any party feeling,—with a complete independence, which shall have the dryness and the detail of a legal document, and which, in proof of the impartiality of the author, should gloss over none of the defects, should tone down none of the blemishes, should travel without relaxation of purpose to the very end of the information collected. Every other method of procedure would be futile, dishonest, opposed to the end in view. The Hero should appear in his completeness, lighted up on all sides by a relentless light; no veil should conceal any part of him; it is the business of others to drape his figure. There must be no reservation in the description of his deeds, but "the truth, the whole truth, and nothing but the truth." He must no longer be lauded with phrases; the truth alone must suffice.

And at a blow the spiteful pamphlets and the imbecile apologies will at once find their refutation. The latter, by their stupidity, are worse than the libels. To measure the Emperor with the same yardstick as an adroit man of business who keeps his books properly and is content with a modest profit on the goods which he retails out; to polish up the sharp edges of his medal to the point of resembling those coins where you can still distinguish the image of a sovereign, without being able to distinguish what sovereign it is; to take away from his character and his intellect all their excess so as to bring down his physical and moral features to an expression respectably commonplace and honestly vulgar, is to understand his nature still less than by attributing to it excessive vices, ambition without measure, even crimes without parallel. At least he would remain great; it would be the genius of evil, but it would still be a genius. It would not be a kind of pupil of the Ghetto, compacted of usury and liberalism.

To those would-be impartial persons who on every occasion run down their fellow-countrymen before strangers; to the moralists of the study, who appear to wish to ignore all the unclean dregs of human existence, and apply to Napoleon a philosophic rule which they have certainly not borrowed from their contemporaries, the facts will supply an answer.

Being suspected of having *hypnotised* myself about Napoleon, I ought, more than any other person, to abstain from all polemics, and to keep back, as far as possible, my personal judgments. I will only say what I have found in the documents, and do not feel that I have the right to give my conclusions. Reserved as were those of a former volume, they called forth criticisms the justice of which I acknowledge. What I put forward is a fragment of an investigation. Judgment can only be given when the whole investigation is under the eyes of the public.

The plan which I adopted of indicating none of the sources on which I have drawn has been vigorously attacked, not only in France, but in other countries. But I still adhere to it. On the one hand, it seems to me useless to make the reader take part in the very long and very complex work to which I have given myself up. On the other hand, the references which I should have to offer would teach no one anything; for the larger part of the documents on which I worked either belong to myself, or form part of private archives. In a short time I shall be in a position to publish, in their completeness, certain of the texts of which I made use. It will then be seen whether they are or are not authentic. In addition to this, with the exception of cases where I am under obligation to be silent, I am ready to give to workers who are interested in the subject all the proofs they may desire. This is the course which I have already taken; and the most critical in the examination of documents have been perfectly contented with my explanation.

Looking at this book, which makes its appearance less than six months after my volume of *Napoleon et les Femmes*, it will perhaps be said that I wished to take advantage of success and to cling to the fashion. As a matter of fact, it is the present volume which ought to have been published first.

During last year, in March and April 1893, a Review printed the three articles which form the woof of it. If I have completed them it has been with notes collected a long time back. I have had no need to borrow from certain compilations which have been placed on sale since then; and I undertake to establish, from motives which will be appreciated, for these studies a priority which cannot be questioned.

As to fashion, I have not the leisure to follow it. It would be impossible for me to improvise a book which, whether good or bad, is the result of twenty years' study. It was not the fashion to declare oneself a Bonapartist at the time when I affirmed myself to be one; and if the fashion passes by of writing upon the Empire, I shall none the less go on with my work. But, however, I do not think that it will pass by, for the reason that I do not think that it is a fashion.

At the end of the second Empire there was a fashion of attacking Napoleon III through Napoleon I; to dispute the origin of his power, to become excited over his religious policy, to deny his military greatness, to put his last campaigns in evidence, and to detail his overwhelming defeat. It was a development of opposition similar to that which consisted in dressing out Napoleon III as Caracalla or as Nero for the amusement of a few *literati* of the Académie. To what this hatred of Napoleon, this contempt for glory, this apology of peace-at-any-price have led us is well known. But this has not reformed the pamphleteers. When the Empire fell there remained the principle of authority, the principle of government, even the principle of unity; all that was Napoleon. It was necessary to demolish him, and they hastened to do it. That meant writing against the Emperor, and the dedications of such books were well paid for. There was on the other side no opposition, no reply; possibly from fear of becoming compromised, possibly rather from ignorance. In the Bonapartist party, those who contested the matter were principally men formerly in office, who were little and ill prepared for those studies which require a special education and careful research. An active life had hurried them on, and the revolution of September gave them their first leisure. No doubt, instructed as they were in their calling, knowing all its possibilities, acquainted with all its secrets, they would have had less trouble than others in going back to the source, and in ascertaining what part the Emperor took in it. If at that time among this body of officials, which was truly excellent, there had been found a few men of good will in each of the branches in which human activity finds its development, and in which the Government ought to make its action felt—bridges and roads, mines, prefectoral administration, finance and justice, industry, commerce, diplomacy—who had investigated by means of actual documents, who had formed the organisation, who had foreseen the development and assured it, who had laid down a rule which was most salutary alike to private persons and to the state, their books would tend to exhibit most forcibly the highest idea which can possibly be taken of Napoleon. Everywhere we should have met with his ideas, his decrees, his universal spirit of classification, and that invariable good sense which protected him at the same time from the quibbles of rhetoricians, the details of fiscal authorities, and the exaggerations of men of literature.

But the men who combine the capability, the instruction, and the experience in a given pursuit are frequently wanting in general ideas, and still more frequently in the taste for writing. They are accustomed to do nothing but that which is immediately useful, the results of which are at once apparent. The papers which are submitted to them set them to work, and they want no other incentive, but they recoil from a speculative work which has not received official sanction. And, again, when it is proposed that they should write a book, a sort of professional timidity stops their pen and paralyses their fingers. They are afraid of saying too much, and, by force of being discreet, cease to be instructive. Not that a few creditable works did not make their appearance at this time; but they appealed only to a special and very restricted public, who only wished to find party politics in these attempts at history.

And, moreover, it was not given to any professional writer to direct that current which, at the present day, leads all minds towards Napoleon. This can be explained. The greater number of men who make books by profession come from the Professoriate, from Journalism, or from the Bar,—those three schools in which the hatred of Napoleon is taught, in which, from calling and from interest, they are constrained to detest him.

Does not Napoleon represent military glory, and do not the men of war, thanks to him, usurp a part of the attention which men of letters consider that the public owe to their work alone? To degrade the army by daily insults, by the declaration, each day repeated, of the same calumnies, to clamour for its abolition, to conjure up the Peace Congress, to foster, by means of international associations, the forgetfulness and neglect of one's own country—is not this the work which prominent philosophers and writers of repute are actively advancing, and is it not by adopting these fruitful doctrines that to-day modern moralists exalt those who have no country, and bring forward apologies for anarchists?

Again, Napoleon represents authority, and no class in the state any longer bears restraint with patience. The relentless laws by which the Emperor muzzled the three throats of the Revolution are not of a nature to be forgotten. He obliged the advocates to defend their clients without insulting either the government or private individuals. He obliged the professors to teach their pupils those subjects which they were paid to explain, without preaching either atheism or contempt for the laws. He obliged the men of letters to respect the lawful government of their country, not to reveal to its enemies the weak points of its defence, and not to corrupt the imagination of the people. Napoleon, therefore, is looked on by all these as an enemy,—he, his doctrines, his intellect, even his person,—and that he has continued to be.

Consequently, nothing is to be expected from professional writers as long as they are recruited among such surroundings. But it was reserved for a man who was neither literary nor an advocate to place the question before public opinion in its true light.

When M. H. Taine added to the pamphlet which he had just printed against royal and revolutionary France, that scandalous portrait of the Emperor which bore the unmistakable character of a libel, Prince Napoleon, in exile, replied by a work of history and eloquence which he called " Napoleon et ses détracteurs." A shudder, as it were, was felt to pass through the public. At last some one had dared to hold up his head and carry the war into the enemy's country. At last the Emperor found in one of his descendants an advocate worthy of his cause. Better prepared than any one else could possibly be for such a work, in that he had presided over the publication of the correspondence; because since his tenderest infancy his mind was simply fed on the traditions and recollections of the great man; bearing in his own person striking features of his physical and moral heredity,—the Prince was one of those whose voice, when he raises it, in spite of the uproar of crowds, carries to the extremity of the forum. In language belonging to himself alone, which disdained the artifices of rhetoric, and never sacrificed the very smallest atom of the sense to the turn of the phrase, he says what he knew and what he thought of the Emperor; and these few pages, passing over the head of the professor of rhetoric who had given the occasion for them, had the result in many hearts of arousing the sleeping passion for the illustrious dead.

The fitting time also had arrived. The twenty generations which, since 1871, had passed under the flag had then learned that which is taught in all the armies of the world—that Napoleon was the greatest man of war of all times. In proportion that our young officers studied the history of the great wars, in proportion that their chiefs rendered themselves capable of teaching them, admiration, respect, passion for the Emperor-chief of the army, absorbed all other feeling. It was no longer for the legend that they waxed enthusiastic, it was for the real and tangible; for they studied it at close quarters, they scrutinised each campaign, each operation, each detail of organisation. The military correspondence of Napoleon was their breviary. Not content with what was printed, they were anxious to learn by actual documents how in time of war, beyond the bold strokes which he carried out, he trained, led, and fed his army; on what information he made his decisions; how he conducted the service of the front and the rear. And after each new publication we were obliged to confess that if France was conquered it was because she deserted his injunctions and others were adopted.

From the officers this veneration descended to the soldiers. What glory was to be spoken of to them to rouse them, if not his glory? What army was to be held up as a model, if not his army? What victories were they to celebrate, if not his victories? Thus, little by little, by the power of facts alone, without united action of any sort, without previous understanding, everywhere throughout the whole army, through which the entire nation passes, light appears.

The military painters, more in touch than any one with the army, were the first to translate into startling representations these thoughts of the soldier. Weary also themselves of depicting for seventeen years the disasters of the terrible year, they desired to break away from it, and went straight to this inexhaustible fountain of glory, in which incidents are abundant where everything is picturesque, both men and horses, and affords materials for interesting compositions. Did they see any farther? No. But in carrying on their profession conscientiously, in executing excellent pictures or wonderful drawings, they discovered that they had helped on the movement which was about to take place in a very remarkable manner. Reproduced in enormous numbers, their pictures succeeded in striking the minds of crowds of people, and when in 1889 the Exhibition of the Ministry of War, on the esplanade of the Invalides, was thrown open to them, what they saw there completed the conversion.

In this palace of a day, thanks to the intelligent initiative of a few members of a commission from which, without doubt, the Minister did not expect so vigorous an effort, were found collected together all the relics of the generals and of the soldiers of that age. Hovering over them, everywhere visible and present, was the image of Napoleon. Of the whole of the national fair, this palace was the most visited. Pouring into it in deep waves, from the very vestibule, the most excited and the most noisy held their peace. A certain religious and sacred feeling entered their troubled minds. They passed along the glass cases silently, deliberately, thoughtfully, and continuously. Of the heads bent down in examination, there was always a varied succession, and always a stream of men, of women, and of children, which flowed by as the months passed. Through all their eyes they drank in glory, the glory of the people, of peasants and workers like themselves, taken away one day from the paternal field or from the workshop, to return after five years all covered with gold, charged with decorations, holding in their hand the staff of a Marshal of the Empire, rich enough to buy provinces, and called by a name new and sonorous, a name of victory which was to them more precious than the name of their father. And him they recognise who, raised far above them all, distributed, as he pleased, fortune and renown; him of whom, in their childhood the old soldiers talked—him whose image they had for so long a time seen above the great fireplace of the paternal cottage,— the Man, the Conqueror, the Martyr; the supernatural being whose misfortunes alone were equal to his pleasures, whose name alone, mysterious and unique, is like a rallying cry, everywhere understood, which unites all people in a bond of admiration and respect.

And then, as if awakened from the silence of the tomb by a Divine law, the witnesses of the epic begin to speak. It was a remarkable occurrence; all other voices, those whose stories the public best loved to hear, whose indecent stress it revelled in, whose prurient details it received with delight, no longer found an audience.

Everything turned towards these phantom mouths, which at last gave forth the expected secrets. And these secrets were those of our passed greatness; confidence in the man of genius, devotion, self-denial; they were vigorous sabre-cuts given or received, strange cavalcades crossing Europe, squares broken with a superb rush, rivers crossed by swimming, adventures more surprising than any novel; and by the light of the fire of cannon, in a fog of powder and bleeding dust, he appeared, his hat over his eyes, in his long greatcoat, unmoved, serene, superb.

And then he was to be seen as he lived, to be followed in his moments of tenderness, and in his misfortunes. We felt for him in the same way as his old soldiers. We learnt again to love him. When during his last days at Saint Helena he inscribed in his will the name of that Marbot, whom he knew for a certainty to be of the number of the brave, but whose talent as a writer had only just been discovered by a *brochure* of a few pages; when "*he would urge him to continue to write in the defence of the glory of the French Armies, and to silence calumniators and apostates,*" did the Emperor perceive that this book of Marbot's, buried for half a century, published almost by chance, would succeed on one memorable day in awakening in all hearts, even in those which were the hardest and the most closed against him, sympathy for the soldiers, a passion for their adventures, respect for their uncomplaining stoicism, and a love, generous and strong as was theirs for him who for twenty years strove for France, and with France, against the world.

All this prepared the movement; but still it was not this which produced it. Under the force of circumstances with which it appears that the recollection of Napoleon had no connection, the Nation suddenly found itself in such a state of mind that a *cultus* of the Emperor was alone capable in its own eyes of consoling it, of fortifying it, and of restoring it. His name was a symbol; he combines the idea of glory, the idea of authority, the idea of honesty. The Nation is wearied of defeats, and longs for victories.

The Nation is wearied of parliamentary anarchy, and looks towards the man who gave them back security and order. The Nation is wearied of seeing the conscience of those who govern it put up to auction, and looks towards him who, inflexible, insisted on restitution from financiers, and emptied the pockets of contractors.

To a people of simple views, a name is necessary to summarise its dream. But for a century, each time that the people, sunk into the quicksands of parliamentarism, feels itself on the point of perishing, at the risk of hurrying on the catastrophe, it makes a desperate effort, in spite of the sand which is closing its lips, and the filth which is filling its mouth, and throws out a last appeal, a last cry, after which nothing remains but death; and it is this man whom it calls to the rescue, it is this name which it gives utterance to as that of the supernatural being who alone can save.

In 1799, when the People wished to free itself from the ignominy of the Directory; in 1815, in 1830, and in 1848, when it attempted to overcome the oppression of the aristocrats and the financiers; in 1848 again, when it was disgusted with republican anarchy, five times already in one century, it was the only name which summed up all the aspirations of the people. But for all, in 1799, in 1815, for the greater part in 1830, for the mass even in 1848, the name was that of a living person, and it was to his genius that the people appealed. At the present day there is no influence of survivorship, no belief in an heirship, no thought relating to any descendant. It is to Napoleon dead, to no member of the Napoleon family living, that the soul of crowds leaps out. Napoleon seems like a creation of the reason, a being of legend and of dreams, so good, so strong, so far superior to surrounding humanity, that, for this nation which has no longer the remains of faith in the ancient gods, it is he who becomes the God.

There is at present no party which can restore him to France; he is too far away in time, too exalted in glory. To her alone can he serve as leader and guide, for she alone is equal to him, and can without failing support the weight of his name.

Vainly, by the side of his worship, is the attempt made to create a rival. Joan of Arc, declared venerable by the Church, after having been condemned by the Church; Joan of Arc seized and monopolised by the Catholics, exalted into a worker of miracles, whose marvellous acts were not only inspired but carried out by a divinity, from that time forth loses hold of the country. The visionary who is guided by St. Michael and St. Catherine, no longer is the representative of the spirit of France, that spirit incensed against the English invader, which descended into the little shepherdess of Domrémy, and to the time of her death animated her sweet and overflowing love for our land. The statue of Joan, which each will honour in his own way, may unite all believers to the country: the shrine of Joan will unite only the believers in a religion.

Joan, besides, however glorious the recollection of her may be, represents only the struggle against the foreigner, the defence of the native land. She is far removed in point of time, and belonged to an age so different from our own, that, saving our country, nothing that touched her and excited her to action suffices to move us. He, on the other hand, is entwined in all our fibres, and there is not an atom of his flesh of which our flesh is not made. He bore our whole social system; he made its laws and its institutions. He impressed on it the form which it still bears, although a century has passed away. He suffered all our miseries; he gave us all our joys. For twenty years he carried on the formidable resistance of France, alone against the whole of Europe. He was the Revolution as far as it possessed sublimity; he was the Country in all that is most sacred, for after all the glories which he gave her, he fell with her, and it was a common disaster which annihilated them,—her for a time, him, as to his sovereignty, for ever.

And let it not be said that it was Napoleon who led France into this disaster. History is there to reply. Valois and Bourbons, the Revolution and the Empire, the Government of to-day and that of to-morrow, have encountered and will always encounter the same enemies, since they will be France, and will concern themselves in her mission, her interests, and her glory. The coalitions which are formed against France are not the consequence of the internal form of government which she adopts. They result from the very configuration of Europe, and from the fact that France will always be looked on with jealousy simply because she is France.

The political system by which the Bourbon kings had been compelled, by the very force of circumstances, to be restrained, which took three reigns and two centuries to form, is —let it be understood—the same system which Napoleon was compelled to adopt; only he effected it in fifteen years. The Bourbons, in order to protect their frontiers, had been forced to constitute the League of the Rhine, to put kings of their own family on the thrones of Spain and Naples, to establish a point of support in Upper Italy, and to endeavour to annex Belgium. What else did Napoleon do?

Was it he who entered into the struggle with England? Putting aside the Hundred Years' War, and the wars of Belgium, let us take history only from Louis XIV. What page of it is there which is not reddened by the English with the blood of France?

War from 1666 to 1667, from 1672 to 1679, from 1688 to 1697, from 1701 to 1714, from 1740 to 1748, from 1755 to 1763, from 1778 to 1783, from 1793 to 1800; in the eighteenth century alone, out of a hundred years, forty-one of open, declared, official war. On the Continent, whoever attacks France has England behind him. Napoleon governs, and the same thing happens as in the time of the Bourbons. It is not the Bourbons, nor Napoleon, which England designs to destroy; it is France.

In these fifteen years is found collected and represented the complete national history. In his own person Napoleon unites the grandness and the disasters of the whole Bourbon dynasty. By him are summed up and united victories similar to Denain and defeats like Malplaquet. In him is embodied at the same time the struggle for the freedom of the seas and the struggle for natural frontiers. Like Henry IV, he brings peace to consciences; like Louis XIV, he organises the administration; better than all the kings, he creates the unity of the nation, and Condé, Turenne, Luxembourg, Villars, Saxe, are soldiers in the past, as in the present are Lannes, Davout, and Massena.

The ignorance of Napoleon brought on France and its army the disasters of 1870; it brought on the nation the orgies of parliamentarism,—that shameless corruption which made of the law-court a public exchange of votes; it brought on the Government such a lowering of the principle of authority that it relaxed all the springs, destroyed the administration, introduced a want of discipline into all its ranks; it brought on society that moral anarchy which rotted and disintegrated the class which professed to direct, long before it had provoked in the class which held no property, and which would no longer be directed, the proselytism of the bomb. That society trembles at present. It was when it threw him over who alone could protect it that they should have trembled. It is astonished at the frequency of anarchist attempts. It is their rarity which ought to astonish. When anarchy is in the minds of the shopkeepers, how should it not descend to the mass of the people? Why should the shopkeepers alone have the monopoly of satisfying their appetites, when the appetites and interests serve only as a base to society, when the principle of authority no longer has its devotees, and the Country even is no more than a figure of oratory which serves to cover all expenses and to justify all peculation?

Country, authority, society—these are what Napoleon represents. He alone supplies us with a common faith and hope, a common religion, a common form of worship. He alone can deliver us from a common terror.

In him alone we Frenchmen—who are not oppressors and are tired of being oppressed—can and ought to meet on common ground. It is because they have known how to honour their heroes and keep them in faithful recollection, that other peoples have become great at our side. A pedant has said that it was the Prussian schoolmaster who conquered at Sadowa. Nonsense! It was Frederick the Great. And it was he, living, who at Sedan conquered Napoleon, dead.

France, lying down in its armour of war, sleeps a heavy slumber, a slumber which has lasted for four-and-twenty years. Around her swarm and buzz the rabble of spouters and betrayed who take her for their prey. They cry and dispute, they howl about figures, they feign indignation, they hiss, they laugh, they amuse themselves. She, while their noise does not succeed in disturbing her dream, sleeps on, dreaming of times past,

INTRODUCTION.

and does not even perceive that they have stolen her mantle of purple to cut it into the shape of the tunics of kings. But let the Hero, so unmoved by these outcries, ascend the mountain, let him appear, and with a gesture he will disperse and overthrow this band of rulers; let him lean over the pillow of the warrior maiden and kiss her forehead, and suddenly she will stand erect, more radiant and more noble, her lance in hand, her helmet on her brow, as she appeared in former times, when, hovering in the blue heaven on rapid wings, she led the pioneers of glory to make their harvest on the plains of Jena.

If he delay, this Hero whom we have expected for so long a time, if death overtake us before his hour, at least out of veneration for this man, who to our fathers was a saviour, let us bring up a generation which shall be faithful to his memory, which shall receive the teaching of his history, and shall grow up in devotion to him. Who knows? Perhaps some child will be discovered, born for glory, who will feel that he is worthy to follow his footsteps, and who by a Montenotte will show that he knows the roads which lead to Marengo.

FRÉDÉRIC MASSON.

March 1894.

NAPOLEON AT HOME.

I.

ETIQUETTE.

A NEW order of things has arisen. A new monarchy is established on the ruins. But can it be called a monarchy?

Doubtless he who now occupies the Tuileries has this in common with his predecessors, that he is an absolute ruler; but he conquered for himself that which was theirs by right of inheritance. If in point of intellect, activity, and genius it is impossible to establish any comparison between him and them—for they only inherited what he grasped by his own power—what imperious authority must he not have possessed to equal that which formed, as it were, an integral part of their personality.

The Most Christian King presented himself to his people encircled with the radiant shades of the kings his ancestors; and these kings were so numerous and so remote that they reached back to the very sources of the nation; they were so closely bound up with it that their name was associated with each occasion of its aggrandisement, of its victories and of its reverses, so that the history of the House of France was the history of France itself. Was it not these kings who, bit by bit, had built up the edifice and, by their laws and their institutions, had so deeply fixed their imprint on each individual that it occurred to none as possible that he could be governed by other methods, so that, for centuries, to rebel meant an appeal from the king to the king himself? As all justice flowed from him, to bring a matter to his notice was to ensure the delivery of perfect justice at his hands.

Before the king, as a rampart, was that innumerable body of gentlemen, attached to him much more by tradition than by interest; compelled to serve in the armies by family duty and by the honour of caste; holding loyalty as so much a matter of custom and so invariable that they looked on it as something to be taken for granted, about which it would have appeared beneath them to take an oath; for they were of the same race as Fabert, and, like him, for the sake of the king they would have put their persons, their families, and all their possessions in the breach. This they testified by their emigration, by their service in the Army of Condé, at Quiberon, and on the scaffold. This testimony of a whole caste in favour of a form of government has no equal among any other nation. To testify to its faith in the monarchy the nobility gave its life, its fortune, the inheritance of its children; it suffered cold, hunger, misfortunes of every sort, misfortunes which, for it, were much worse than death; this it did after centuries of power and of opulence, at a time when it seemed to be enervated by success, by an over-refined civilisation, by alliances with those beneath it which it had been compelled to make in order to keep its position. To cure itself of the vices to which it had fallen a victim, the call of duty, clear, strong, and distinct, sufficed, for the surface only was sullied; the heart beneath the robe of silk remained the same as beneath the armour of steel, and honour did not call on it in vain.

Side by side with the nobility, the clergy

imparted to the king—a bishop outside the Church—the immeasurable power of a religion voluntarily allied with the monarchy. Having espoused its claims and adopted its principles the two became so intimately united that the subordination of the Church to the temporal head of the nation became in the eyes of its spiritual head the safeguard of his liberties. There was no dispute among the priests on the origin of the civil power, no discussion as to the form in which it was exercised. God Himself was proclaimed the founder of royalty, and the decrees of the sovereign dropping from the seat of Truth were almost regarded as matters of faith.

Then came the Third Estate, attached to the monarchy by thousands of offices of finance and judicature, by thousands of little honours to which it might hope to attain by purchase or gift, rising step by step, generation after generation; and these aspirations prompt it to keep its place in the State or at Court. A whole hierarchy separated it from the king, but the hierarchy had steps which might be mounted. There were cases of commoners who, in the time of the kings, gave their orders to men of the sword, and became the ancestors of dukes and peers. To what did not Finance lead if it could only marry off its daughters? What could not the Parliament do for him who had obtained an office? The nobility held the sword, but the Third Estate possessed the money; it bought everything that was to be sold, and many things already were on sale. No doubt the Third Estate had its detractors, but they were so few in number that they scarcely counted. To make them numerous it required the confusion caused in secondary education by the abolition of the Company of Jesus. So long as these results did not ensue, the ambitions of the Third Estate prompted it to line its pockets if among the farmers-general; to push itself forward if engaged in the Palace or in the Administration; and if unconcerned in such matters, to gain position in its native town, its guild, its corporation, or its profession. Its vanity waited only for letters patent to consider itself on a footing with the nobility. Envy alone made it a leveller, but the king was too exalted to be envied.

Such was the surface: beneath, it possessed great virtues. In the first place, the sense of respect; then the instinct, the taste, and the passion for becoming rich and of rising in the world, patience, frugality, and honesty. It was in no hurry, and was content to work for the future.

To a king who knew how to humour him, he did not refuse to lend his money, provided he was satisfied that he got something in exchange. He but rarely gave his blood, because he could make no profit out of it, and because that was the business of a gentleman; but let him be ennobled, and he will show that courage is learned much more quickly than fine manners. The less important the privileges which he has won, the more he holds to them. If they are touched he is incensed. It is not he who of himself caused the Revolution; at the outset he followed in the wake of a few broken and bankrupt nobles who showed the way; then he seized his own advantage, but only because the king and the nobility gave up the struggle. To induce him to wish for a change, and then to work for it, it was necessary that those whose whole interest was to avoid a change should be the first to preach it; that those who had to watch over the principle of authority should employ all their weapons to destroy it. Up to this time the real Third Estate was passive, and took no leading part in the movement. A constitutional monarchy would have completely satisfied it, because in that form of government it foresaw its own access to power. For the king, whom it looked on as outside the question, it preserved, after three years of Revolution, a sort of respectful devotion. From 1792 to 1798 three electoral *coups d'état* were necessary to put an end to the expression of its loyalty—the massacre of September, the 13th Vendémiaire, and the 18th Fructidor. The Third Estate, as well as the nobility, had its defections; but these, in neither case, were entitled to speak for their order, which they had disowned, and which disowned them.

The Third Estate as a body was Royalist, and remained so.

Below the Third Estate, still lower down, was the People, who on solemn occasions, to the sound of peals of bells, through a golden dust, surrounded by glittering steel, got a glimpse of a supernatural king, loaded with gold, resplendent with precious stones, who passed like a flash of lightning, drawn by eight horses in a coach of gold. No near approach was possible, nor contact even by chance, except on the day when that king, the elect of God, returning from the altar and consecrated with the triple anointing, touched with his hand the hideous wounds of the poorest of his subjects, and cured them. He appeared only on religious festivals, or in military ceremonies: in the former as the priest-king; in the latter as the inheritor of conquerors, the chief and leader of the men of the sword, the heaven-appointed defender of his people.

That part of his every-day life which he had in common with ordinary beings had no existence for the crowd; such a notion was lost and stifled in those impenetrable walls which separated the sovereign from the multitude, and within which were fenced off the different classes of people of the court. There remains a being, very great, very good, and very just, whose will is law, who lives in a palace of gold, eats, drinks, sleeps, rolls in gold; a being whose remarkable longevity in two instances makes the reign seem eternal, without beginning, without end. From 1643 to 1774, in a hundred and thirty years, were two kings only ; two kings who bore the same name, both of them Louis; so much alike in face that one might be taken for the other. Is it not always the same—a king who ceases to have an identity and becomes only THE KING? Hence an excess of veneration, a sort of annihilation before that master who is more than human, whose existence is exempt from ordinary laws, who is so far off, so lofty, so like a god.

Now, nothing retains its existence! Everything which has formed the object of respect, the consolation, the ambition of past generations, is scouted, vilified, shattered, destroyed ; their very names execrated. No more laws, but at the caprice of Assemblies in a state of frenzy ; decrees repealed almost as soon as they are passed, and as to which it is a question whether the penalty of death is the punishment for obeying them or for disobeying them. No more national institutions, but in turn England, Sparta, or Rome has become the model ; no more morals, but the despotism of depraved instincts ; all classes of society, all ranks, all professions, all degrees of fortune shaken as in a winnowing basket by some gigantic winnower, deaf, blind, and mad; prostitution rendered lawful by divorce; the family suppressed, friendship proscribed, modesty dead; and the only master of everything, the only sovereign of living beings, alone respected, alone worshipped—Money; money which has taken the place of God, of the king, and of the nobility, which alone confers every right, usurps every privilege, is the cause of every act of tyranny, corrupts every mind, and which of that France, given over to stock-jobbers, to thieves, and to bankers, makes an immense market-place where everything is for sale—the country, justice, law, honour, everything except glory.

The man of glory has appeared, who after the ten years during which parliamentary despotism, and the anarchy of the sovereign Assemblies lasted, humoured the disgust of the people; the roll of a drum, the display of a few grenadiers in the orangery at St. Cloud, and all was over; and at the same moment money recognised its master, him whom alone it could not buy, for all the gold in the world could not purchase Montenotte or Rivoli.

But to reconstruct a France, nothing— nothing but those ragged togas soaked with gore and mud, which, in the park where the Five Hundred have thrown them away in flight, make here and there a red spot which still resembles blood. With nothing a nation was to be restored; to that end give back Faith which makes priests, Honour which makes soldiers, Honesty which is the bond of individuals and of civilised nations. Before everything, and as a beginning, it was necessary to restore that principle of authority which for eighty years past kings, queens, ministers, and courtiers, as if in emulation, had been so relentless to discredit and destroy, before even it had fallen so low as to be the prey of imbeciles, incapables, and madmen.

But how was this principle of authority to be restored to that pitch of power which it naturally possessed under the kings? No doubt the general of Italy and of Egypt brings his great personal influence to strengthen the supreme magistracy with which he is invested; no doubt it is founded on the unanimous suffrage of a nation thirsting for security for the present and for some time to come; no doubt his person is adored by the army and by a portion of the people; but how little does this amount to in comparison with that aggregate of power which the last of the Bourbon kings possessed, virtually without any trouble to themselves, by the mere fact of their birth, which, in spite of their mistresses, and their wives, allowed them to reign for sixty years.

To the principle of authority as represented by Bonaparte a divine institution is wanting; it does not carry with it the nobility, whose loyalty is incorruptible; it is wanting in that majestic remoteness, that retreat into time and space, which make of the sovereign, who has become as it were a creature of the imagination and of dreams, the inevitable, unquestioned, irresponsible, the almost impersonal master of his people.

It was only by degrees that Napoleon broke through these limitations, and only in proportion to the increase of his power. At the outset a magistrate appointed by the people, and sharing, at least nominally, the exercise of the sovereign power, he was, by the express terms of the Constitution, only one member of a government, appointed for ten years; eligible for re-election indefinitely, it is true, but subject, in the same way as his colleagues, to that necessity of re-election which is the true characteristic of a republican form of government. His new form of authority could have nothing in common with royalty; its legal power had its origin in the sovereignty of the nation, and in fact it is the army, that is to say, force, which established it; it is by the consent of the people, and by force, that it is maintained.

Even when, two years after Brumaire, Bonaparte had freed himself from the uncertainty of re-election; when, by being appointed consul for life, he had obtained all the prerogatives of the sovereign with the exception of heredity, he is still only a magistrate. The foundation of his power remains the same; his rank is not indelible, his authority is subordinate. When even the last step is reached, and when, like the ancient kings, he has mounted the throne and has encircled his brow with a crown, he has still to acknowledge an external power higher than his own, and if in the executive formula of his decrees he abandons the precise words *Will of the People*, he is constrained to recognise that he is *Emperor by the Constitutions of the Republic*, which implies the recognition of all the degrees of the national sovereignty.

He who has a sovereign above him, even if it be the people, is not a sovereign. The authority, therefore, with which the emperor is invested is far removed from that of kings. However despotic it may be, although it may override all control, although it may act most rigorously, it will never possess that potential energy which the royal authority enjoyed; it is no longer possible; the Bourbons themselves, if they could return, would be powerless to recover it. The Revolution broke the charm; it broke through prescriptive right; it showed that kings could be overturned; it left in its wake an indefinable trace of scepticism; it abolished reverence, and by those oft-repeated oaths which it exacted in favour of so many varying constitutions, it destroyed the feeling, even the very idea of fidelity. Henceforth treason ceases to be treason so soon as it becomes a matter of politics, and in order to violate his solemn faith, every man finds in his conscience arguments which will absolve him, and allow him to keep his place and to serve, one after the other, with equal zeal, all the successive forms of government. Louis XVIII, on his return, would have done well to date his first Royal Act as the eighteenth year of his reign, and thus by the only logical means to have established the legitimacy of his authority; he would have done well to place himself above facts simply to affirm the right; he would thus have proclaimed to the world that he alone represented and embodied that right, no longer believed in. Was he still able to believe in it himself?

If the sovereign authority was unable to regain in its integrity the prestige which naturally attached to it before the Revolution, at least, in becoming emperor, Napoleon attempted to restore, as far as was compatible with the spirit of his time, the two elements which he judged essential, not only because they formed the support of the Bourbon monarchy, but because they were of necessity the foundation and the safeguard of all hereditary monarchy.

The necessities of his throne were a supernatural origin, and a body of men around him who, owing the satisfaction of their ambitions and of their desires exclusively to the new order of things, should devote themselves entirely to him. He required lastly a distinguishing mark which, in the eyes of the people, should place him in the same rank as the overturned throne of the ancient national kings, or as the existing thrones of neighbouring kings. Singular difficulties arose; Napoleon wished to follow no foreign model. He was compelled to seek his example in national history. This the later kings could not furnish him with, for they were the summing up of the successes of their ancestors; in their case the dynasty which they represented was the creator of its own definite form; they were the outcome of centuries. Napoleon was the founder of his own dynasty. It was the founders of dynasties alone, therefore, in whose steps he could follow.

Of these there were two: one was simply a great lord, elected by lords his equals; his power was limited by the oligarchy of whom he was the representative, and whose privileges he engaged to protect. No resemblance existed between the position of Napoleon and that of Hugues Capet, and it was not from the Duke of France developed into the King of France that an emperor could draw his inspiration.

The other had the recommendation of the services of his father, but possessed no hereditary right. He was not the chosen of a few, but the elect of the whole nation, or of that part of the nation which carried arms, which alone counted: in that way he became Cæsar. Nevertheless, he did not look on his reign as assured, his dynasty as founded, until the Pope, the interpreter of God and the arbiter of spiritual authority, had poured on his head the holy oil, and placed on his brow the crown. This consecration he might have demanded from the bishops of his empire, but he wished to receive it from the head of the Church, from him who binds and who looses, and from whom, in the eyes of all Christians, every truth emanates.

Here was the example. The similarity of the situations is striking, and forces itself on the mind. Napoleon inherits no recommendation from his father, but possesses the recommendation of his victories. He was the elect of all, of the people and of the army, and he is Cæsar; but, like Charlemagne, he does not hold that national election takes the place of supernatural origin. By the two Concordats he had re-established the Catholic religion in France and Italy; in doing this he considered that he was yielding to the wishes of the two nations, whom he was justified in supposing Catholic. Like Charlemagne, therefore, it was from the Pope, and from the Pope alone, that he could claim investiture. He will thus clothe his authority with the divine origin which is wanting to it, and, reascending the course of ages, will unite the fourth dynasty to the second.

It is on this account that Napoleon is continually referring to Charlemagne, that he proposed to dedicate to him a gigantic monument on the Place Vendôme, that he erected a statue to him at Aix-la-Chapelle, that on every occasion he insists on his admiration for the great man for whose relics at Aix-la-Chapelle he was anxious to show his veneration so soon as he became emperor. Perhaps some tradition of the Carlovingians, his ancestors, still excited the great admiration he bore for his august predecessor; perhaps some tradition of the Byzantine Emperors, handed down in legend; but a glance at history served to establish such strange coincidences between his own destiny and that of Charlemagne, that he was led, indeed compelled, to seek no other model.

He too fills the place of lawful kings, and claims to substitute his dynasty for theirs; he too, with his eyes fixed on that Italy which he has twice conquered, looks on his empire as incomplete unless he reigns over the people of the Peninsula at the same time as over the French; he too has seen all the Germans of the East rise in arms against the principle which he represents, and his lieutenants went to the places where Charlemagne fought in order to quell their revolt.

When Napoleon says, "I am Charlemagne, because, like Charlemagne, I once more unite my Crown of France with that of the Lombards, and because my empire reaches to the East," the cry comes from his heart. It is from the imperial costume of Charlemagne also that he copies his coronation robes; it is the coat-of-arms attributed to Charlemagne, a golden eagle on a blue field, that he takes for his bearings; it is the imperial *insignia* of Charlemagne, the crown, the sceptre, the sword of Charlemagne which Kellermann, Pérignon, and Lefebvre bear before him on the day of his coronation.

If not from Charlemagne himself, it is from the Holy Roman Empire founded by him that he borrows the greater part of the titles with which he invests the great dignitaries of his empire. Cambacérès is arch-chancellor of the empire, because there was in the College of Electors an arch-chancellor of the empire, who was archbishop of Mayence. Lebrun is arch-treasurer, as was the Count Palatine of the Rhine. Louis is constable, not because a constable up to the time of Louis XIII commanded the armies of the King of France, but because a constable was one of the Palatines of Charlemagne. If the name of Grand Admiral is without precedent in the Germanic Empire (for even in France it dates only from Louis XIV and brings to our recollection only the Comte de Toulouse and the Duc de Ponthièvre), it is in accordance with German traditions that the dignity of grand elector was taken; and it is again from the Holy Empire that we get those deputies who were appointed to supply the places of the great dignitaries; there are a vice-grand-electeur and a vice-constable in the Napoleonic Empire because in the Holy Empire there were a vice-grand-master of the Palace, a vice-grand-marshal, a vice-grand-chamberlain, and a vice-grand-treasurer.

As far, then, as possible, in the great dignities of the Empire, Napoleon copied, if not Charlemagne directly, at least the successors of Charlemagne. He follows the same course when, with a view of surrounding the fourth dynasty with a devoted body similar to that which the Bourbon kings possessed in their nobility, he institutes the Legion of Honour, and the nobility of the Empire. With the latter the similarity is remarkable. Like Charlemagne, Napoleon has his dukes and his counts; he contemplates the creation of margraves. When he admits barons and *chevaliers* it is because the two titles are in use in the Holy Empire; if he creates princedoms (Essling, Eckmuhl, Wagram,) it is not until 1809, at Vienna, following the example of the Emperors of Germany. And lastly, when to the son for whom he hoped, he assigned, even before he married Marie Louise (*Sénatus-Consulte* of February 17th, 1810), the title and honours of King of Rome, what more convincing proof can there be that the thought of Charlemagne and of the Holy Empire haunted him incessantly? Was it not in Germany that he found the title of King of the Romans given to the son of the emperor, to the emperor who was not crowned ? And in the statement of the grounds of this *Sénatus-Consulte* of 1810 does he not make his orators say, " Napoleon, in the first days of his glory, abstains from entering Rome as a conqueror. He waits till he can appear there as a father. It is his wish in that city to have the crown of Charlemagne placed on his head for a second time " ?

Complete as Napoleon dreamt the identity to be between his empire and that of Charlemagne, there were many points in which he was constrained to depart from the model he had chosen ; for to satisfy the largest possible number of his companions in arms he was compelled to multiply offices, and in a lower rank than that of the great dignitaries—of Carlovingian origin—to create other great officers, having, for the most part, no duties to perform, whose titles could only have relation to institutions which were in existence recently, or which could be created anew without ridicule.

The twelve Marshals of the Empire (*twelve* as soon as Murat and Berthier were promoted to be grand dignitaries) have by their very number some air of resemblance to the twelve peers of Charlemagne; but the five colonels-general of cavalry, the inspectors-general of artillery and of engineers, and the four inspectors of the coasts, had no counterparts before the Valois and the Bourbons.

These offices were purely ornamental, and these "grand officers" of the Empire would not, any more than the "grand dignitaries," have daily duties to perform in the service of the Emperor. Their posts formed the excuse for large salaries, splendid uniforms, and nothing more. On days of ceremony the "grand dignitaries" and the "grand officers" of the Empire would take their places in certain rooms apart; they would form the *cortège* of the sovereign or would surround his throne; but they knew not how to direct the Court, nor how to superintend the various services of the Emperor's house so as to give to both of them the dignity and the splendour which Napoleon desired.

It became necessary, therefore, on this account to have special officers who should be "grand officers of the Crown." If these important posts received from him the same titles which they bore at the Court of the Bourbons, it is for the reason that in every monarchy analogous duties must have similar titles. Everywhere the "grand master" or the "grand marshal" assumes the general direction of the household; the grand chamberlain has charge of that which belongs to the chamber or the wardrobe; the grand almoner watches over the spiritual department; the master of the horse directs the stables; the grand huntsman manages the hunts.

In different countries other accessory offices are created according to the wants of the service, or the requirements of politics and of finance. Thus, we saw in France a grand butler, a grand cupbearer, a grand pantler, a grand falconer, a grand master of the wolfhounds, a grand cook, a grand master of the woods and forests; but with the exception of the grand huntsman and the grand almoner, which in several states are not found, we find everywhere these three offices essential to the state of the monarchy and to the majesty of the throne—the grand master, the grand chamberlain, and the master of the horse.

These, then, Napoleon was of necessity bound to re-establish; not a "grand master," for the title is too ambitious, but a "grand marshal," as in Germany; a grand chamberlain, and a master of the horse, for no Court was without them. He appointed a grand almoner because such an office was customary in France, a master of the hounds for the same reason, and, with equal rank, a grand master of the ceremonies, whose office is still more necessary than in former times, for all the new-comers have to be taught an etiquette which many have forgotten, and which most have never known.

Napoleon thus places himself on an equality of state with the other sovereigns of Europe; he constitutes his Court essentially of the same elements which form theirs. The customs of Courts are everywhere the same, so that, willing or unwilling, he is compelled to accept the traditional way of naming these offices which existed at the Court of the Bourbons, which alone adapted itself to the times in which he lived—for in truth the days of Charlemagne were somewhat remote. Having re-established these titles, what duties shall he assign to their bearers? How shall he contrive to conciliate modern feeling, the spirit of equality, the spirit of the Revolution, of which, in spite of all, he is the representative, with a ceremonial the hatefulness and absurdity of which he recognised? His aim was not so much to surpass in splendour the kings who preceded him and the sovereigns who were his contemporaries; it was especially to restore to the embodiment of authority all the splendour with which it was surrounded before the Revolution; it was to attach to his new government a considerable number of ambitious men who, of their own accord, would come and occupy the positions he had designed for them, and who, to recover the titles which they had borne, or to receive similar titles, would abandon their ancient masters; it was to promote expenditure by the festivities which he would command, and thus foster national industries; it was to re-establish a centre from which should radiate an example of politeness, of manners, and of fashion; it was lastly, by the numerous barriers and the distance placed between the emperor and the people, to increase the veneration of the multitude. But there is a wide distinction between such a course and any attempt to re-establish the power of the great officers of the Crown, and their subordinates, on the same footing as under the Bourbons, or to resume the etiquette practised fourteen years previously, and to insist on its strict observance. If he desired to do so it was impossible.

The etiquette, at which people who considered themselves emancipated might smile because they had lost the intentions of the ideas which it symbolised, was not formulated at a single stroke; it was the product of the experience of ages, the rational application of traditions, many of which reached back to the very founders of the dynasties, while some were even more ancient than the dynasty itself.

France had had neither the privilege nor the special burden of etiquette. In it, etiquette was the law of the Court as it is the law of the Court of every monarch by Divine right. To make a joke of it, to ridicule it, to abolish it, give the popularity of a day, but overthrow a monarchy of twenty centuries. To act like Louis XVI, shows the most complete misapprehension that a king can have, both of the character with which he is invested and of the conditions which allow him to exercise his power.

The law of etiquette was not the invention of Louis XIV; he only adapted it to his kingdom by the introduction, according to precedents, of certain prescribed forms; but if the principle was differently carried out according to the usages of nations, it was virtually identical in Spain, in England, in all the German monarchies, in Turkey, in Persia, in the Indies, in China, in Japan, in every place where a monarch reigns who claims to hold his power from God.

The sovereign by Divine right could only be approached by those of the nation who had been raised to the highest dignity. These are his witnesses and his servants; they assist at and take part in all the acts of his existence. They are the intermediaries between him and the nation, and render him services, which, servile in themselves, take the character of the highest honours when his person is in question. They are under obligation to render them, but it is also a right, and the sovereign cannot recede from it without falling short of his character. The two terms are inseparable.

If it is a privilege to approach the sovereign —a privilege dearly bought, for in addition to the questions of birth and position, every place, in France at least, involves its money value, which is considerable—it is necessary that the duty of every post which gives this privilege should be performed personally by its occupier, and that regularly and punctually, whether important or otherwise; so that every courtier must consider himself infinitely honoured by the office which he fills, by the fact that his duties compel him to be in the presence, and he must be so deeply devoted to the interests of the sovereign that he can imagine no other ambition than to serve him, nor conceive any other desire than to please him, nor form any other project than to advance in his good graces. This faith in the monarchy must spread through every courtier to the public, so that every man who gets rich, or who rises in the world, shall not think himself satisfied until he has gained possession, by his money or by his sword, for himself or for his descendants, of some place in which he can personally serve the king.

In order that each of the ceremonies which

form the reason for the presence of each of the officers of the household may be duly performed, it is necessary that the life of the sovereign should be laid out to the minute; that the sovereign should never be wearied nor bored by being thus waited upon; that he should feel so deeply the inmost nature of his quasi-divine mission, that none of these attentions should weary him; that he should bring to it the conviction that he is not performing vain ceremonies, but acts of a lofty importance. In this way every one is satisfied; from it the king draws the power of faith in himself; for it he is more respected, and this respect increases his importance in his own eyes; the officers of his household feel themselves honoured in serving him, consider themselves the foremost members of the state, and if they give themselves up to intrigues to obtain the favour of the sovereign they are not dangerous to the throne; the nobility and the upper middle class aspire to offices which can be multiplied indefinitely, and which are an inexhaustible resource for the treasury at the same time that they form the goal of all ambition; the very people, knowing that the sovereign is waited on by the most illustrious families of each province, for that reason acquire more veneration for this master of masters.

For the existence of an hereditary monarchy it must unite in itself these three elements: the sovereign must be convinced that he possesses in his own person the fulness of law; those who surround him must be convinced that as the sovereign is the embodiment of law, to approach him in order to render him the most humble services constitutes the highest distinction; his subjects, all his subjects, must be convinced that the sovereign could be no other person, that he is *because* he is, that he has had, so to speak, no beginning, so old is his dynasty, and that he will have no end, so surely is its heredity assured.

Etiquette alone ensures these three elements: by confining within the Court the material life of the sovereign, it becomes surrounded with a sacred mystery; it is from this mystery that its power proceeds, and it is the reason why, little by little, except in the case of the very greatest, the absolute sovereign becomes unapproachable; his face can no longer be looked upon; those even who are admitted to his presence must not lift their eyes towards him. Everything depends on this, it all hangs together. The Oriental despot who lives shut up in his harem, whom none of his subjects have ever seen, whose presence is only revealed to the ambassadors of foreign nations by the rhythm of traditional music, or by the barbarous clang of brazen gongs, is alone logical. He is God's envoy, or he is God; and God is invisible.

In Europe, because the dynasties are there too young, and probably for that reason alone, kings have not driven logic quite so far, but they would have arrived at that point if they had lasted. In France ceremonies had already acquired such an importance that they engrossed nearly all the hours of the day; and each was necessary, not so much because tradition would have it so, but because the existence of the ceremony had caused the creation of a whole group of offices which would not have been filled up if the king had got rid of it. When the Revolution redeemed or abolished the offices, the ceremony fell into disuse. The tradition nevertheless remained: was it really the sovereign unless he was surrounded by the same crowd which in former times surrounded the king, unless the same ceremonies were performed? How, on the other hand, was it possible to have the courage to submit to them? How was it possible to have the endurance to support, day after day, such servitude? How was it possible to yield to that series of obligations which up to the last days of the Bourbon monarch, accompanied, for example, so simple an act as the *Lever*?

The first *valet-de-chambre*, who slept in the king's chamber, calls in the *garçons de la chambre*, who quietly open the shutters and set the door ajar for the *entrées familières*; then, the king being awake, the *grande entrée* is summoned; the king getting out of bed, the grand chamberlain, or the first gentleman of the chamber, hands him his dressing-gown: then, after intervals, all duly prescribed, the grand master of the wardrobe puts on the night-jacket and the blue ribbon*; at each ceremony of the toilet a corresponding *entrée*: the first *entrée* or *entrée des brevets*, *entrée* of the *ambassadeurs de famille*, *entrée de la chambre*, the fifth *entrée*, which is performed when the king has washed

---

* The order of the Holy Ghost.

his hands, the sixth *entrée* when his majesty has taken his shirt. It seemed as if the *entrées* were from one of Molière's pieces, from one of the *divertissements* of the *entr'actes*, and that the courtiers ought to advance dancing and with graceful gestures. In truth, they almost did dance, and the whole ceremony was like an *air de ballet*,—of a religious ballet, very measured and solemn, as the priests of all religions dance before their idols.

It is a special prerogative to pour spirits of wine on the hands of the king, or to hand him the holy water vase, to undo the right or left sleeve of his night-shirt; it is an honour to pass the king his shirt, an honour which at first fell to the sons or the grandsons of France, then to princes of the blood, then to legitimate princes, only in default of these to the grand chamberlain, afterwards, following the order of rank, to the first gentleman of the chamber, to the grand master of the robes, to the master of the robes, to the officers of the wardrobe, each in his order; and this shirt, warmed, covered with white taffety, is, according to the rank of him who is to give it, presented by such a person whose duty it is, taken in the prescribed manner, so that the king behind his dressing-gown, held up by two *valets-de-chambre* to conceal him from observation, may be left to shiver while such or such a one coming into the room draws off his gloves and puts himself into the posture of waiting on him.

Imagine Napoleon subject to such constraint, and waiting like this for his shirt! If even his inclination would allow him to submit to such trifles, how could he find the time?

His life is far too much taken up by work to allow him to waste hours every day. Besides, in this palace, still riddled with the bullets of August 10th, where the floor is still red with the blood of the murdered Swiss and gentlemen, how was it possible to take up the whole of the cast-off clothes of kings? Are there not patches which on them keep up a traditional majesty, which on another would look like the disguise for a carnival? For such ceremonies to make any impression, to provoke respect, to assure the dignity of the throne, or at least to retain their seriousness and to be received in that spirit, they must have some sense, they must be founded on tradition, they must call up old memories. In this case there is nothing of the kind—no tradition save that of the Bourbons, no memories apart from theirs, nothing which in itself can belong to the new dynasty.

For the establishment of a form of worship priests must be found, and these priests must have faith in the religion the mysteries of which they celebrate. But it was impossible for Napoleon to have that inward assurance of his sovereignty which was possessed by the kings descended from Hugues Capet. In his case etiquette was a necessity of the monarchy, but could not be an article of faith. As it applies to himself it is an organisation which he insists on, a law which he enacts. But how many enactments have fallen into oblivion in ten years, how many laws have been revoked! The etiquette which he proposes to lay down will be obeyed, for force is on his side, but it cannot be respected. The men who have sprung from the Revolution will take it seriously as far as it affects themselves, but in no respect as it affects others; the men of the *ancien régime* will see in it only a parody of that which has passed away. It will not even be in their eyes an etiquette in the proper sense, that is to say, a code of ceremonial, each clause of which is constituted by a precedent, each precept justified by an example; it is simply an order which will last as long as he who gave it.

To restore the ceremonial of the monarchy in its integrity was not to be thought of; not that Napoleon feared by adopting it to render himself ridiculous (he had no sense of the ridiculous; he said himself, " Power is never ridiculous "), but he would not restore it because it would worry him, and, moreover, he could not because he was not surrounded by the large number of persons necessary to carry it out in such a manner that he might not be inferior to the ancient kings.

His companions-in-arms do not excel in such duties. Their rides through Europe with death on the crupper had not given their backs sufficient suppleness for the duties of the antechamber. They knew not how to fulfil them, and committed all sorts of blunders. It is from birth itself that such habits are acquired, and the whole education must be given with that object.

Even those younger men who have not arrived at the highest rank, and who up to now formed the Consular " family," men of dexterity and men of brains, are almost useless for it. Without looking at their origin, without troubling himself from what stock they issued, and from what college, Bonaparte recruited them by the chance of the times, for their good looks, because he had seen that they were brave, intelligent, and honest, these at the siege of Toulon, those on the day of Vendémiaire, some on the staff of Berthier, others on the battle-field of Marengo : a few are noble, but very few, and of the smaller nobility who had never approached the Court. One alone is of good family, but it is precisely his name, much more than his military reputation, which caused his promotion to the staff in the last days of the Consulate.

As for the Prefects of the Palace whom he appointed about the same time to do the honours of his receptions and to take care of the contents of the palace, they were but simple major-domos, of a position a little better than servants, but of whom the best connected were members of some family of finance, while those best instructed in etiquette had already filled some menial office in the Royal Court, some purchased place which allowed them to add to their patronymic the title of some estate, and at the end of two or three generations to deck themselves out with an assumed title and with a name to which they had no right.

The great nobles, really of ancient nobility and really of the exalted race who had been the grand officers of the Crown of France, were not to be thought of. Those who had not perished on the scaffold remained in exile religiously faithful to their deposed but not uncrowned king. The grand almoner of France, the Cardinal de Montmorency-Laval, lived at Altona; it was useless to speak of the grand master, the Prince of Condé, of the grand chamberlain, the Prince de Guémené, of the master of the horse, the Prince de Lambesc, of the master of the hunt, the Duke of Ponthièvre, princes of the blood royal, or of the House of Lorraine. The grand butler, the Marquis of Verneuil, was dead; the grand pantler, the Duke of Brissac, had been murdered; the grand falconer, the Marquis of Vaudreuil, was by the king's side; the grand master of the wolf-hounds, the Comte d'Haussonville, had scarcely returned from emigration. He died in 1806, and it was only four years later, in 1810, that his son offered himself as chamberlain.

There were no first gentlemen of the chamber, no captains of the guards, no governors of the royal houses; none of those were to be found strolling about the Tuileries in the year XII—neither Richelieu, nor Durfort, nor d'Aumont, nor Fleury, nor Noailles, nor Luxembourg, nor de Poix. Much more than is supposed, the high nobility remained faithful to its masters: for appearance' sake Napoleon was able later to recruit a few starving younger sons; but the heads of the names and arms, of those who had charge of the family, he could not have gained over so soon, even if he could ever have done so.

Without the unremitting participation of this illustrious body, the restoration of the ancient etiquette was impossible; these men alone possessed the secrets of it, they alone knew the details. Alone they had succeeded for ages in placing themselves between the king and the people, without a murmur from the latter, because the people knew that they were illustrious, and that the splendour of their services exalted the majesty of the throne.

There are reasons of another order, which, disregarding the *impossible* which he would never take into consideration, must have presented themselves to Napoleon's mind and have determined him.

The ancient monarchy rested on a dynastic fiction. The new was entirely founded on the idea that the nation chose its chief. The royalty of the House of Capet supported itself by mystery, by the ignorance in which the people remained as to the value of its king; the Empire lived by the constant intercourse between the emperor and the soldiery, and by the conviction which all the citizens had formed of his genius.

Bourbon France remained as it was, because ages after ages had so moulded it; because each king had added his stone to it, because each queen had brought her dowry; because each of the peoples which formed it, in submitting to the sovereignty of the king, whether accepting it or protesting against it, had preserved its own institutions; because these little nations, of which the king was the sole bond which united them, preserved their particular habits of life, their ways of thinking, their language, their customs; and although the attempt had been made, they had never become united into a single and grand nation. They possessed no unity of mind, no similarity of aim, no uniformity of laws. The King of France, who was in fact only king of the Isle of France, ought, as other sovereigns still do, to have added to his title, if it had not been, as was said, the highest after that of King of the Heavens, the enumeration of the duchies and of the counties of which he was the lord. In this way he would have proclaimed an absolute truth. He alone gave an apparent cohesion to these various elements; in him alone were united the rights which he held much less by conquest than by the assent of the heads of the people. To him alone, not as king, but as duke or count, could be traced back the feudal hierarchy of each duchy and of each county. To disturb a capital was to put the whole edifice in danger, to upset the whole arrangement. The faith of the times must be accepted, holding that that which had taken six hundred years to organise, and which for two centuries had acquired its definite form, would still last for many reigns.

The machine being thus set up and almost in working order, it was necessary to let it go on as it could, without pretending to do away with useless wheelwork, or to replace what was worn out with new. Consequently every one had his place, and each institution, however superannuated it seemed, had its purpose, its utility, its necessity. In order that people should preserve their respect for it, that they should not see the cracks in it, and that by some whim they should not be tempted to demolish it, it was necessary that this immense and singular piece of mechanism, all covered with dust and rust, should be in some measure lost in a sort of foggy and golden atmosphere, in which objects became confused, so that the imposing and majestic mass was alone visible. As soon as kings reduced the thickness of the veil which covered them, respect disappeared. As soon as they touched the machine to repair it or to improve it, the machine stopped. There is a time when the foolish wheels still turn in the void, but the mainspring is broken. Soon all that heap of corroded ironwork and of rotten wood falls to pieces as of itself, at the risk of crushing the entire nation, and the earth for some distance is strewed with the fragments.

But the people rouses itself, takes courage, and wishes to live. From duchy to duchy, across overturned barriers, they address each other, and are surprised that they understand. They soon advance to meet, recognise each other and embrace. They have the same hatreds, the same wants, the same interests, the same ideal. And from one end to the other of this kingdom which had nothing in common but the king, men of a different race, who express themselves in different dialects, feel a similar thrill pass through them. They wish to be a nation, and they are France.

Of this nation Napoleon is the elect. He has constructed his own machinery, to his own satisfaction and to the satisfaction of France. It is new and solid, and loses nothing by close examination. The springs of steel which he has picked up here and there on the ground he has tempered anew for his own use. He has combined them with wheelwork which seems new, with all of which, however, the nation itself has provided him. He has been careful to work up into it nothing foreign, holding that the country suffices for itself, and should not live by borrowing. He has made his machine high enough and wide enough to rule the world, delicate enough to adapt itself to every new necessity. A wheel ceases to work—it is removed; a spring is worn out—it is changed; and the machine continues to go on. The machine is independent of him. He is its supreme mover, but he is not its indispensable mover. No doubt for its full action it is necessary that the chief of all should be the elect of all; but even if he is displaced from that foundation, even if the crowning part is taken away, the machine works on.

As far as it concerns himself, he feels that it is to this single principle, that of the sovereignty of the nation, that he owes his existence. If at times he wishes to make no distinction between the dynasty he established and that of the Bourbons, if in a way he accepts their succession, if he forces himself to give to his own sovereignty a similar outward appearance, nothing could take away the necessity of remaining in touch with the nation. In those hours when his power appeared to be established so firmly as to defy every storm, he was able to multiply the intermediaries, to appear no longer before the people except surrounded by gorgeous pomp, in imperial costume, even to increase the mystery surrounding his person and to shut himself up in his harem. But when the bad days came and the European coalition threatens him, he goes of his own accord to invigorate himself among the people; he shows himself to them in military costume, frequents the streets and market-places, appeals to the familiarity of the nation, so completely does he feel that " all power emanates from the people, and that nothing done without it is lawful."

For these reasons, therefore, he is of opinion that, as in the case of those sovereigns who preceded him in France, as well as of those who reigned around him in Europe, it is necessary for his *prestige* to form a Court and to institute a code of etiquette. He recognises at the same time that the restoration of the ancient Court and the ancient etiquette would be impossible; his disposition could not adapt itself to such trammels, nor could his work be thus interfered with. Such a course was clearly impossible and would be dangerous and injurious. It was necessary in this as on other occasions to adopt a middle course, that he might be a *conciliator* as he had proved himself in legislation, in home and foreign administration, in the control of religion, in the management of landed property, and in the settlement of personal property. He must still draw up a definite scheme—one which shall combine the past with the present, and impart to the new monarchy which he is creating both the brilliancy which he aims at and the splendour with which he aspires to surround it, as well as that connexion with the past which he thinks necessary, and which at the same time shall secure to him a comparative independence of action. This arrangement should permit the sovereign to preserve the freedom of his private life and his public work ; should keep him in permanent contact with the army, and should, lastly, allow him frequent opportunities of intercourse with the nation, so that he should be informed of the great movements which arose, that he might receive the special requests which the citizens had to make, and thus might be in a position to repair injustice, and the misconduct of his agents.

This formula Napoleon hit upon, and we may almost say that he did so without groping about, and at the first attempt. He recognises two beings in his own person: one, which in physical, intellectual, and moral process has wants which must be respected, for which complete liberty is necessary; the other is under the control of his sense of dignity, and directed by the grand master of the ceremonies, a creature of spectacle and pomp, whose steps are governed by etiquette, and who, as soon as he makes an official appearance, is subject to all the ceremonies customary among absolute monarchs. The man retains his right to think, to work, to live as he would, to act as he pleases; the sovereign preserves the surrounding necessary for his dignity, but from this surrounding he only accepts symbolic services which are the representatives only of those real duties for which originally every office was instituted. It is this which Napoleon was fond of stating, saying that "he was the first who had separated the *service of honour*" (an expression coined in his time) "from the *service of necessity*; that he had put aside all that which was real and menial, to substitute for it that which was only nominal and purely decorative."

He founded this innovation on the following

reasoning: " A king," said he, "does not exist in nature, he exists only in civilisation; there cannot be a naked king—he is only a king when he is dressed." True for him, the theory was false as far as concerns kings by Divine right. No doubt they do not exist in nature, but it is because they are above nature. Their power is supernatural in its origin and by its transmission. It is thus at least that they look on themselves, and thus that those around them understand them. It matters little whether they wear the badge of their dignity or not—their character is indelible. It is independent of the exercise of their power. It does not depend on the coronation which most of them received at Rheims: the coronation is for them only an investiture, it is only a consecration. Naked they are kings to the full as much as clothed, and the domestic duties which the great ones of the kingdom perform in dressing them or undressing them assert without contradiction the permanence of their monarchical power.

In the case of Napoleon, on the contrary, his character is new, he is dependent on a triple investiture — military, national, and religious. In the past he is connected with nothing, in the future he leads to nothing. The honours which are shown him are addressed to the sovereignty with which he is invested—a sovereignty the badge of which he ought to wear—not to the man who reserves the right to have a private life, an unofficial life, without failing in his duty as sovereign, without falling short of royalty as did Louis XV, and still more Louis XVI.

Possibly this distinction did not present itself to the mind of Napoleon, or more probably he did not, even at St. Helena, wish to express it because it would have been the avowal that so far his power was inferior to that of the Bourbons; but it is the result of the facts, and he was unable to escape from it. When he said, "If I had been my grandson!" and considered what would have been the extent of his authority if he had held it for no more than two generations, he affirmed, and with remarkable vigour, how far tradition was wanting in his monarchical edifice; how far, as soon as he quitted the reality of democratic right to seek for sources of Divine right, he found himself inferior to those whom he replaced, for in that he who would not recognise the impossible, knocked his head against something which was outside him and above him—Time, which alone consecrates dynasties and gives them in the eyes of the people an air of divinity.

To reconcile that which forms the reality of his power with that which up to that time had been the representation of it, the emperor is therefore compelled to have two existences: one, of parade, has for its stage the "*Appartement d'honneur*," and the State apartments of the palaces, the chapel, the theatres, the Corps Législatif, the Sénat, Notre Dame, and the Hôtel de Ville, all the different scenes where he had to play in public the part of emperor; the other, his real life, his personal life, his life as a man, his life as a worker, his life of husband and of lover, flows on between the walls of the "*Appartement intérieur*." There he is himself; he appears with his familiar habits, his methods of work, his passion for order and arrangement. It is there that he must be seen if we attempt to represent the man that he was capable of being, and if we wish to form a notion of his normal existence—that which enabled him to be equal to his work and to fulfil his destinies—if we wish to form a notion which approaches at all closely to historical truth.

II.

THE APARTMENTS. THEIR PROTECTION.

TO form a notion of the habits of life and the familiar manners of Napoleon in his private apartments, the best plan, no doubt, is to take the apartments of the Tuileries as a type, and we are called on to reconstruct these apartments entirely by means of documents of indifferent authority, or insufficient for the purpose, in the almost complete absence of actual representation. No more than the shadow of the Palace remains in which one can seek for the shadow of the Emperor. Napoleon, indeed, spent days at Compiègne, at Rambouillet, and at Fontainebleau, but scarcely more numerous than at Schönbrunn or at Potsdam; from these places no more particulars can be gathered than from the head-quarters at Marrac and at Mayence, or from the imperial palaces of Strasburg and of Bordeaux. It was, in fact, at the Tuileries and at Saint-Cloud that he lived longest, and each of these places is now a blank.

It may be said that, on an average, from Floréal of the year XII to April 1814, the Emperor's official residence was at the Tuileries for nearly three months a year. This does not mean that he never left it, nor that he slept there every night; without being a wanderer like Louis XIV, or still more Louis XV, who was always transferring his dulness from Versailles to Marly, to Choisy, to Saint-Hubert, to Bellevue, to Compiègne, to Fontainebleau, Napoleon was far from settled. When evening came he would decide suddenly to start for Malmaison or Saint-Cloud, would go occasionally and establish himself at the Elysée, would start off and pass a day or even a night at one of the châteaux which he had given to his companions of war,—Grosbois and Grignon, for example; and this was not noticed in the official reports of his movements, it was not even in the early times entered in the *Journal des Voyages*. It used to be said, especially at the beginning of his reign, that he wished to keep his household perpetually on the alert, to accustom it to change quarters at once, and that it pleased him to add to the difficulties of the Grand Marshal and the serving people. In fact, it satisfied his craving for continual activity and movement. But go where he would, he liked to find the rooms arranged in the same order as at the Tuileries; he wished his private apartment to be similar, with furniture made on similar patterns, and arranged in the identical positions. As soon as his necessaries were unpacked, his portfolios open, he at once became at home; he had everything he required at hand, for no man had fewer different wants, fewer fancies, or was more regular. That which formed the familiar surroundings of his life was contained in a few chests—one might even say in a few small boxes—and, however great might be his magnificence, however much he desired to clothe his surroundings with grandeur, there remained in the Emperor much of the *sous-lieutenant* of former years, ready to start when the trumpet sounds to horse, and only wanting a few minutes to cord his baggage. Thus his palaces have always the air of an inn. All his personal belongings follow his person, and when he has left there is no trace of his passage, nothing to indicate his tastes, nothing to show his character or his habits. Beyond his cipher on the furniture and hangings, his coat of arms, the bees which have taken flight from his imperial mantle and settled here and there on the walls or on the floor, nothing recalls him. From motives of economy, and also because there was nothing better, nor as good, to be done, these seditious badges were at a later time covered with a shred of cloth, and kings followed each other in the use of this imperial furniture without much embarrassment, for nothing of the spirit of the first occupant is to be discovered in this furniture.

He took possession of these apartments in the same way, and with as little fuss, as though he were going into one of his head-quarters, Osterode or Finckenstein, the Escorial or the Kremlin. In every place he was at home—in the house of Louis XIV or in that of Philip II, in the house of Ivan or in that of Frederic. His maps spread out, his great table placed on trestles, he set to work, without the necessity of any familiar surroundings to bring back the current of his thoughts. That mattered little to him He had a mania for order, but it was satisfied at a very slight cost ; it aimed at what was necessary, not at what was superfluous. He thought nothing either of the richness of the furniture or of the sumptuousness of the decorations, but much of the arrangement of his actual tools, indispensable either for his physical existence or for the production of his brain. It is for this reason that in his apartment the arrangement, which he had himself drawn up and which was contrived so as to be identical in whatever place he went to, for which a few screens sufficed, gives much more insight towards a knowledge of the man than the decoration of the rooms ; and that the positions occupied by the pieces of furniture in regular use reveal more than the description of the furniture itself. The latter does honour to the maker, the other shows a manner of life.

At the Tuileries—and it was the same in the other imperial residences—the portion of the palace assigned to the habitation of the sovereign was distributed into three descriptions of apartments :—

The apartment of ceremony ;

The ordinary apartment of the Emperor ;

The ordinary apartment of the Empress ;

The first two only concern us here.

The grand apartment of ceremony was reserved for fêtes, ceremonies, assemblies, and grand audiences. In the every-day life it was not made use of. The first room was a concert hall—the Salle des Maréchaux—which, taking up with the grand staircase and the grand vestibule the whole of the central *pavillon*, formed the communication between the two wings of the palace; that on the left, containing, in two stories, the apartments of the Emperor and of the Empress; and that on the right, in which were situated the hall of the council of state, the theatre, and, further on, in the *pavillon* of the "Enfants de France," in the façade looking on the Rue de Rivoli, the apartments of the Grand Marshal and of foreign princes.

In leaving the Salle des Maréchaux, the first room of the state apartments, one came to a first and second *salon*, the throne room, and then the *salon* or state cabinet of the Emperor, and finally to the Gallery of Diana. The state apartments ceased there.

Similarly situated to the Gallery of Diana, and having its private entrance by a staircase near the " Pavillon de Flore," stretched the *appartement ordinaire*, itself divided into the *appartement d'honneur* and the private apartment. The *appartement d'honneur* consisted of a guardroom and of a first and second *salon*. The private apartments, which were in continuation, comprised the Emperor's study, an interior study, where in the morning Napoleon gave audiences, a room which was used as a topographic office, a small bath-room, a bedroom, a dressing-room, a wardrobe, and an antechamber.

This suite of rooms was repeated by a similar suite in the story above, composed of an antechamber, of a dining room, of a work-cabinet, of two *salons*, of a bedroom, of a boudoir, and of a wardrobe. This suite is often called the *appartement secret*; it was called officially by the name of the "Petit Appartement de sa Majesté," and could only be reached from the inner suite of rooms.

To get a clear idea of an arrangement of this kind, which is remarkably difficult to describe, the strangeness of which a plan, however exact, would scarcely explain, the best course, now that the Tuileries are destroyed, is to pay a visit to the small apartments at Versailles. There, in those dark corridors, where two persons can only pass sideways; in those narrow staircases, which turn so sharply, and which must be lighted day and night; in those rooms so small and so low that the head touches the ceiling—these rooms in which Louis XV, Louis XVI, queens, dauphins, princesses, favourites of all descriptions, passed their lives, it is possible to understand what the Tuileries might and must have been.

At one of its extremities, as we have seen, the *appartement intérieur* was separated from the staircase of the " Pavillon de Flore " by the guardroom, which was occupied by the pages on duty and by a *sous-officier* of the *garde-à-cheval*; from this opened the first *salon*, into which entered, of right, the colonel-general on duty, the state officers of the crown; in it remained on duty the *aide-de-camp* of the day, the chamberlain of the day, the *préfet*, and the equerry on duty; and here were received persons admitted to an audience, or summoned to work with the Emperor. It was the *salon de service*. The second *salon*, communicating on one side with the cabinet of the

Emperor, on the other with the *salon de service*, was devoted to audiences. In the doorway of each of the *salons* stood an usher; at the door of the guardroom was a doorkeeper, armed, as a matter of ceremony, with a halbert and sword.

At the other extremity of the *appartement intérieur*, to the antechamber of which access was gained by passages and staircases leading from the extremity of the Gallery of Diana, an usher, of extreme trustworthiness, kept the door. Within, a keeper of the portfolio, who was a sort of clerk, and a *valet-de-chambre*, remained at the disposal of the Emperor. There was no other guard. In the apartments there was not a single soldier. The only guard which was posted in the interior of the palace, called the guard of the guardroom of the state apartments, was in the right wing, beneath the staircase of the *Salle du Conseil d'État*. It was there specially to give the salute, and was composed of only twenty men. The only sentinel posted inside was under the central *pavillon*, in which there was a public passage to the court and garden. There was, besides, a guard of forty-one men at the *Pavillon de Flore*; a guard of twenty men at the swing-bridge; a guard of twenty-one horse soldiers, furnishing two *vedettes*, at the gate of the *Carrousel*; a guard of seven *gendarmes*, and a guard of nine *pompiers*; but none of these hundred and eighteen soldiers entered the apartments.

It is true that in addition to the five door-keepers, the ushers, and the *valets-de-chambre*, *adjudants supérieurs*, *adjudants* of the Grand Marshal, and *adjudants* of the palace kept up a continual watch; but little by little their number was reduced within surprising limits. Under the Consulate there were at first twelve officers, from the rank of chief of brigade down to that of captain, who had the title of *adjudants supérieurs*. There were still twelve *adjudants supérieurs* to be found in the year XII—three generals, six colonels, two *chefs de bataillon*, and one captain; but when the Empire came these twelve were dispersed among the different palaces as governors or under-governors, and those who remained in the service did not exceed four in number. In 1807 they received the title of *Adjoints du Palais*, and disappeared in 1808, to be replaced by two marshals of the lodgings and four quartermasters of the palace. To the *adjoints* and to the quartermasters are to be added the governor of the palace, whose duties were almost honorary, and the *sous-gouverneur*, when the place was filled up, and the *adjudant*, and we have the entire body to whom the Emperor confided the safety of his person.

All these were men of extreme trustworthiness: of the two *adjoints* of the Grand Marshal, who possessed the rank of colonel, one, Reynaud, was an exceptional soldier, of unequalled bravery, covered with wounds, who had made all Bonaparte's campaigns, and who, having risen to the rank of general, and having been sent to Spain, had the bad luck in 1811 to be taken by the insurgents; the other, Clément, beginning life in 1782 as private in the regiment of Neustrie, had been promoted by the First Consul to the staff of Desaix at the same time as Savary and Rapp. His duties at the palace did not prevent him from having his thigh broken by a bullet in the campaign of 1805. He was a Republican, a self-made man, agreeable, polished, and well brought up, and, like Reynaud, absolutely devoted to the Emperor.

Philippe de Ségur—who, both as a general and as a writer, deserves a special notice in the history of these times—was appointed in 1802. He had the rank of Captain. The First Consul had him summoned to Saint-Cloud. "Citizen Ségur," said he to him, "I have placed you on my special staff. Your duty will be to command the guard which keeps watch over me. You see the confidence which I place in you. You will warrant it. Your merit and your talents promise you rapid promotion." Ségur, who was already devoted to Bonaparte, and had joined the hussars as a volunteer in the campaign of 1800 (whose father, among the first to come over, was *Conseiller d'État*, under the new form of government, till he received the appointment of Grand Master of the Ceremonies), was both astonished and overcome by this confidence, and to his last hours he deserved it.

The fourth *adjoint* of the Grand Marshal was named Tascher, a cousin of Joséphine, and although the Emperor had no great opinion of him, in five years (1803—1808) he made him pass through all the ranks to that of *chef de bataillon*. In sending him to Joseph, who took him for *aide-de-camp*, he wrote that "he may get practice and training, and become good for something." We know not if he profited by the lesson, but he got on. Colonel in 1808, Count of the Empire in 1810, General of Brigade in 1814, he succeeded in everything; for if his Empress cousin failed him in France, he had in Spain married a Clary, and that could not fail to give him a social standing. Having, therefore, been slighted, he attached himself warmly to the Bourbons, but enjoyed their favour for a short time only, having died of illness at the beginning of 1816.

The Governor of the Tuileries was changed too often to gain complete authority. Caffarelli was the first, but he became Minister of War and of the Fleet in Italy; Fleurieu was the next, but he received it as a sort of retirement after his unfortunate tenure of office at the *Intendance générale*. The last was d'Harville, who, on the occasion of the divorce, had just relinquished the post of *Chevalier d'honneur* to Joséphine, and in the sinecure of the Tuileries, protected from his importunate creditors, gave himself as little trouble as possible.

The brave *sous-gouverneur*, General Macon,

performed his duties for too short a time. Although appointed on the 29 Brumaire, year XIII, he went through the campaign of 1806, was summoned by the Emperor to undertake the government of Leipzig, and died there, of putrid fever, October 28th, 1806.

He was not replaced as *sous-gouverneur* at the Tuileries, where the whole of the responsibility devolved on the adjutant, Augustin Auger, a remarkable person, who, during forty-seven years of military service, may perhaps have seen fire during riots in Paris, but never went on a campaign. A *chasseur* in Hainault in 1768, then *garde-à-cheval* in Paris, he entered in 1789 the paid *garde-parisienne*, was Lieutenant of the 1st Battalion of Light Infantry in 1792, Captain of a squadron of cavalry of the Department of the Oise in 1793, Captain of the Guides of the Army of the Interior in the year IV and the year V, then Captain in the *garde-à-cheval* of the Directory. He passed into the *garde des consuls*, where he was promoted to be *chef d'escadron*, and appointed *adjudant supérieur* the 15 Germinal, year IX. From that time he was attached to the palace of the Tuileries, which he did not leave till August 27th, 1815, and then only to die two months later.

Auger therefore was the ruling spirit, and it was he who was really the commandant of the Tuileries from 1804 to 1814; from July 18th, 1808, he was assisted by the four *fourriers* of the palace, Deschamps, Baillon, Picot, and Emery, who all came from the *gendarmerie d'élite*, where they were lieutenants or quarter-masters; they had all four earned decorations for their good services, and had proved by their devotion that they were worthy of their distinctions.

During the day, *adjudants*, *adjoints*, or *fourriers* made frequent rounds in the uninhabited parts of the palace. They did not go, however, into the *appartement ordinaire*, which the officers on duty sufficed to guard. It might be supposed that the latter were not called on for active service, but this would not be true. In the year XI a man in private dress entered the first antechamber. Questioned by the officer on duty, a captain of *Voltigeurs*, as to why he kept his hat on, he suddenly drew from under his great-coat a sabre, with which he attempted to kill the officer. The latter put himself in an attitude of defence and pinned the madman against the wall. Those in the neighbouring rooms rushed in hastily, and recognised the man as an old quarter-master of the *Guides*, to whom some injustice had been done, and who, mad with exasperation, had come with the intention of killing the First Consul. He was taken care of and cured, the matter was hushed up, and Bonaparte settled a pension on his would-be assassin.

At night the guardians were scarcely more numerous. But it must be remarked that at this time the palace was only separated from the public garden by a simple terrace of no great breadth, and raised only three or four steps. If then a sentinel failed in his look-out, an evil-disposed person could easily climb the walls and get into the apartments. For this reason precautionary rounds were increased. One night Ségur found on a window-sill a man who was only waiting for a suitable moment to slip inside. This was the only serious alarm, and except for Ségur it would be still unknown. Another time, after a state reception, a man was found hidden behind the

ARRIVAL OF A COURIER.

curtains of the state cabinet. It was a poor madman, an old chimney-sweep at the Tuileries, who imagined that he should discover the soul of his father in the fires or the lights. He was taken to Charenton. These are all the incidents recorded; in spite of the facilities which they would have met with, none of the conspiracies formed against Napoleon aimed at attacking him at the Tuileries, so great was the conviction that he was well guarded. We have seen that this was not the use he made of his army.

At night no more than during the day did the rounds enter the *appartement ordinaire* of the Emperor. The *aide-de-camp* on duty slept there, in the *salon de service*, his head leaning against the door. Some time later an orderly officer and a page were added. In the rooms immediately outside the *salon* there slept a brigadier and a footman. In the *appartement intérieur*, near the door slept a mameluke; another *valet-de-chambre* and a *garçon de garderobe* had their chair-beds in little dark closets. To gain access to the Emperor when some urgent dispatch arrived, the *aide-de-camp* knocked at the door against which the mameluke lay. The mameluke opened it, passed in the *aide-de-camp*, and shut it again carefully, " so that the *aide-de-camp* might be satisfied that no one could have followed him." The *aide-de-camp* then scratched at the door of the bedchamber. This door was shut inside ; the Emperor got up and opened the door only when he had recognised the voice. These precautions, as he had specially explained to his brother Joseph, were minutely observed. " They give no trouble," said he, " and succeed in inspiring confidence, apart from the fact that they may in reality save your life."

During nearly the whole reign the precautions thus established seemed to suffice. In May 1806 a considerable number of the body-guard of the old King, who had not emigrated, and having received employment had given proofs of zeal, requested to be attached to the person of the Emperor, and to be reconstituted as before. Napoleon refused their services. " It did not seem to him suitable ; " but as they were people of honour he sent them to Naples to his brother Joseph, recommending them warmly. At a later time, in 1808, when

Jerome was thinking of establishing a bodyguard, the Emperor wrote to him: "I do not think that you ought to have a body-guard; it is not the etiquette of our family." But on December 30th, 1812, possibly after having stated the services rendered during the retreat by the *Escadron Sacré*, and especially to guard himself from the consequences of an attempt similar to that of Malet, the Emperor dictated the following note: "It is considered that the *Garde Impériale* is not sufficiently brilliant, and that its uniforms and decorations do not come up to the splendour and majesty which ought to surround a sovereign. It is considered that the gates of the palace and the doors of the apartments are not sufficiently guarded, either because the ushers and porters do not do their duty, or because they are not armed as they should be. It might be well to consider a plan for the formation of companies of *gardes-du-corps*, which, while they act as a real guard, would also serve as a training-school for officers of the army. A plan might also be drawn up for the formation of one or several companies of door keepers, who would perform duties similar to the Hungarian *garde-noble* at Vienna, or the Hundred Swiss in Saxony. They should receive a handsome uniform. The *gardes-du-corps* might have cuirasses."

This scheme was studied with attention by Duroc and by Clarke. The Emperor had it brought under his notice several times, and had several draft decrees drawn up by which everything was arranged to the minutest detail,—the constitution of the body, the uniform, the duties in time of peace and of war, the privileges of the officers and of the guards. But little by little, in view of the urgency of the situation, the idea was modified: it was no longer a question of body-guards "furnishing a post in the first room of the apartments of the Emperor, of the Empress, and the King of Rome," it was a question of soldiers providing their own kit, to whom as an inducement for serving, and for joining the army immediately, special advantages were promised. From what happened to General de Ségur it may be asked whether as body-guards the *gardes-d'honneur* would have really presented the guarantees of fidelity and devotion which the Emperor sought.

This scheme took nine years to draw up;

for in spite of what certain witnesses have said about it, it is doubtful whether, although planned a long time back, it was, as is said, the fear of making the Imperial Guard discontented which caused it to be constantly postponed. The Austrian marriage and the attempt of Malet suffice to explain, but not to justify it. No cases exist where body-guards have prevented a popular revolution from making its way into a palace, but there are cases where the body-guard itself has made a revolution in the palace.

III.

THE TOILET.

THE bed-chamber of Napoleon changed its shape and size several times by taking in certain adjoining space, but it always occupied essentially the same position. During the Consulate Bonaparte did not occupy it. He shared the room of Josephine, which was situated on the ground floor and communicated by a narrow and dark staircase with the *appartement intérieur*. Having made up his mind during the early days of the Empire to have a separate room, Napoleon, on his departure for the campaign of Germany, gave orders to have the room which was to serve him as a state bedroom enlarged and decorated during his absence, for it may be supposed that he very frequently occupied in preference the bedroom in the *entresol* of the *petit appartement*.

The work was pushed on actively by Fontaine and Percier, the architects of the palace; they covered the walls with rich hangings of Lyons brocade, strained on panels enriched with gilt ornaments; carved pilasters framed the openings and filled up the angles. The ceiling, painted and gilt, showed in the covings figures of Jupiter, Mars, Minerva, and Apollo, painted *en grisaille*, with raised mouldings of gold on a ground of lapis-lazuli; the armorial bearings and the cipher of the Emperor, with military trophies and garlands supported by winged genii, formed the ornaments of the borders. The bed, raised on a platform covered with velvet, occupied the floor of the room opposite the windows.

There was scarcely any furniture: arm-chairs of gilt wood, covered with Gobelins tapestry, a sort of large English chest of drawers, with brass ornaments, and nothing else.

Between six and seven o'clock in the morning the first *valet-de-chambre* of the Emperor entered the bedroom. Madame de Rémusat has said that "the awakening of Napoleon was generally sad and appeared painful; that he often suffered from convulsive spasms of the stomach, which brought on sickness." "*His awakening was cheerful*," says Marchand; Constant, Roustam, and all those who were in his service speak in the same way. It must be supposed that Madame de Rémusat, who appears so well informed, must have found herself there after a bad night.

The power which Napoleon possessed of sleeping at will, of sleeping for only six hours, —whether he took these six hours successively or by intervals,—is recorded by all those who approached him, as well as the faculty which he had of passing at once from the deepest sleep to the most lucid wakefulness. Both these qualities are common to many men of his temperament.

Napoleon, when he was suddenly woke up, joked for a moment with his *valet-de-chambre*. "Open the windows," said he, "that I may breathe the air God made." Although chilly indoors, the Emperor liked the air; he had a horror of bad smells, and of "closeness"; the smell of paint made him ill. And this passion for fresh air in the morning is characteristic of his sensations of smell. The only perfume which he liked in his rooms was that of aloe wood; no doubt he brought this fancy back with him from Egypt. It remained with him till death, and he was always throwing ayaloudjin on small perfume burners to purify and scent the rooms in which he lived, and where, till very late in the season, there was a fire.

The first *valet-de-chambre* during almost the whole Empire was Constant Véry, who, in the first instance, replaced Ambart, who had become too old and a trifle silly, and had retired with a pension and the post of *concierge* at Meudon; and then Hébert, also pensioned with the *conciergerie* of Rambouillet and 1,200 francs a year. Constant was a Belgian; he was born December 2nd, 1778, at Peruwelz, a *commune* which afterwards formed part of the department of Jemmapes. His father, who kept an inn at the baths of Saint-Amand, agreed, if the story is to be believed, to entrust him to a visitor at the baths, a certain Comte de Lure, who undertook charge of his education, but emigrated and left him behind. Constant attempted to get back to his native village on foot, but found it in possession of the Austrians. He was picked up by a certain Commandant Michau, who took him into his service; he then became servant to a merchant named Gobert; at last, thanks to the acquaintance which he had made with a valet of Madame Bonaparte, he entered her service while the General was still in Egypt. When Eugène returned from Egypt, Josephine placed Constant with him; she then took him back into her own house, and, finally, on starting for Marengo, the First Consul attached him to his person. From that time until the month of April 1814, it may be said that Constant never left Napoleon; he boasted of having had only two holidays—one of three days, the other of a week. It is very probable. He was replaced, as is well known, in 1814 by the admirable Marchand, whose fidelity and devotion to his proscribed master make him one of the most interesting among the exiles of Saint Helena.

Constant, although he was very moderately educated, wrote a "round" hand, and was ignorant of orthography, was very wideawake, and kept himself well informed as to all that passed, thanks to his friend Veyrat, Inspector-General of the Police, who sent daily by his hands to the Emperor a report intended to check that of the *préfet* of the police. Constant took notes, by means of which the bookseller Ladvocat had memoirs drawn up, which, if they ought to be consulted with caution, furnish a quantity of authentic traits to any one who knows how to make use of them. When, however, Constant complains of the want of generosity of the Emperor towards him, he seems a trifle ungrateful. In addition to 6,000 francs wages and 2,000 francs for his dress, a suite of seven rooms, a table of four covers, carriage and horse and a coachman at his orders, the right of entry to the four State theatres; in addition to the indemnities which were assigned to him when he went with the Emperor on campaign and travelling, Constant received from Napoleon, from 1808 to 1814, 1,800 livres *de rente*, an annual pension of 6,000 francs, and sums amounting in all to 261,000 francs. This did not prevent him from deserting at Fontainebleau, carrying off, the Emperor said, a great deal of silver and jewellery.

The first *valet-de-chambre* wore a French coat of green cloth with facings and collar enriched with gold embroidery, a waistcoat of white kerseymere, black breeches, and silk stockings. With some difference in the embroidery, the ushers, the *valets-de-chambre* of the toilet and of the *appartement*, and the wardrobe men wore the same costume. Constant insinuates that this uniform was not obligatory for him, and that he often wore what he pleased. This is possible.

As soon as the room was aired, the Emperor, who got up immediately and wrapped himself in his dressing-gown, received the correspondence from the hands of his private secretary. He sat down before the fire, and opened the letters himself. Those which were of any interest were put aside to be taken up again at leisure. The others, of no importance, were scattered over the carpet, and he called that "his answer." He then ran through the newspapers; those narrow and scanty journals, the columns of which he alone filled, and in which the smallest paragraph which he had not sanctioned caught his eye. He then asked the names of those persons who were waiting in the first *salon*, and mentioned those whom he wished to see. The Master of the Wardrobe, who, as part of his duty, was present at the toilet, and the Grand Marshal, entered without waiting for orders; the architect Fontaine, and Barbier the librarian, were often summoned; and, on their proper days, Corvisart, the first physician, and Yvan, surgeon-in-ordinary.

Of the medical staff these were all who appeared, although since the rise of the Empire it had been organised on a complete scale, and from year to year had been greatly extended. The physician-in-ordinary, Jean Noël Hallé, scarcely ever came again after the day when, at the toilet, the Emperor took it into his head to pull his ears. "Sire, you hurt me!" said Hallé, with temper, leaving the room quickly. A member of the Institut, and professor at the Collège de France, he nevertheless continued to appear in the lists for an annual sum of fifteen thousand francs.

The doctors on quarterly service, two at first, afterwards four, all at salaries of eight thousand francs, followed the Emperor on campaign; they went by his orders to give their attention to those of the sick in whom he was interested, but at Paris they took their orders from the first physician. As to the four consulting physicians at three thousand francs, and the oculist, they were simply honorary.

Of the surgeons, who were more numerous, Yvan only appeared; so that neither Boyer, first surgeon, with a stipend of fifteen thousand francs, who was created baron in 1810, with an allowance of four thousand francs, nor the five surgeons on quarterly service, at a stipend of six thousand francs, nor the four consulting surgeons, at three thousand francs, appeared at the palace. The surgeons on quarterly service followed on campaign, and several of them had by their devotion deservedly received the legion of honour. But on the contrary the doctors, who in the absence of Corvisart gave their attention to the Emperor, approached him only exceptionally, Yvan accompanying him everywhere. This Yvan (Alexandre Urbain) had been attached to General Bonaparte since the campaign of Italy. As early as at Milan his wife appeared at the Serbelloni Palace in the *salon* of Madame Bonaparte, while he was prancing in the staff of the General. From the year VIII he was so far looked on as a friend as to be almost alone admitted to sign the marriage contract of Caroline. He had, besides a yearly stipend of twelve thousand francs, the post of surgeon-in-chief of the Invalides, the gold cross of an officer of the legion of honour, the title of baron with an allowance of nine thousand francs, without taking into account fees which yearly varied from twenty-five to thirty thousand francs. At Fontainebleau, on the evening of March 14th, 1814, after having put him down for forty thousand francs on the list of the two millions, the Emperor gave him two hundred thousand francs and the cross of commandant of the legion. Some hours afterwards, Yvan, in a state of madness, went down to the stables, took a horse, and made the best of his way to Paris. Napoleon did not forgive him.

Of all the doctors the only one in whom Napoleon had confidence was Corvisart. "I have confidence in the medical skill of my first physician Corvisart," wrote he to Mme. Montesquiou in 1812. He had felt it ever since the Consulate, when, on the recommendation of Mme. Lannes, Joséphine induced Napoleon, whose health had been for a long time out of order, to see him in consultation.

Corvisart, at that time forty-seven years of age, was in full possession of the reputation which he had acquired at the Clinical School of La Charité by his new methods of investigation. He applied them conscientiously to the examination of the condition of the Consul, examined with the minutest care all the organs one after the other, and discovered that Napoleon was suffering from an eruption driven in, which badly treated had brought on a considerable falling away and disorder in the lungs. "It is nothing," said he: "it is a humour driven in which must be brought out." He applied two blisters on the chest, which became less oppressed; the cough disappeared little by little; and, struck by the simplicity of the means employed, as well as by the accuracy of the diagnosis, Napoleon attached Corvisart to him as his only doctor. (Barthez had the title, but he lived at Montpellier, and when Napoleon assigned him a stipend it was in recollection of his father, Charles Bonaparte, whom Barthez had taken charge of in his last illness.) From the early days of the Consulate down to 1814 Corvisart was therefore first physician, with a stipend which amounted to thirty thousand francs a year, without speaking of an allowance of thirty thousand francs attached to his title of baron; he was none the less constantly in want of money, however extensive his practice was in Paris. Married during the Revolution to a girl of noble family, by whom he had a son whom he wished to legitimise, he lost the child, and as soon as possible obtained a divorce to resume a bachelor life. Court life did not please him, and the official world had no attractions for him. He passed his leisure time at the house of his old friend Guéhéneuc, who, as well as he, loved rough pleasantries; or in a society still more gay, in which he met vaudevillistes such as Barré and Desfontaines; the ballet-master Despréaux, the husband of Mme. Guimard, a number of *bons-vivants* and pretty women. Ravrio, the dealer in bronzes, who composed songs in his leisure, sang the virtues of the doctor—

"Quelquefois gai, toujours paillard,"

and celebrated the recollections of the little *fêtes* in which Corvisart took part. They were of a somewhat rough kind.

Corvisart, then, scarcely ever appeared at the

toilet except on his days of duty, Wednesday and Saturday. Napoleon received him with jokes: "You there, great quack! have you killed many people to-day?" And Corvisart replied in the same cue, allowed his ears to be pulled and rubbed, knew how to profit by an opportune moment to make a request, and was one of those through whom a number of alms passed.

Nor did he disdain any more for himself the gains which he drew from his office, for he had a passion for curiosities and rarities, for pictures and objects of art. His patients of both sexes did not allow him to be in want of them; witness that marvellous snuff-box with an ancient cameo, a present from Joséphine, which, bequeathed by Corvisart to Mme. la Comtesse de Soulès, and by her to Professor Jules Cloquet, appears as No. 5,293 in the collections of the Cluny Museum; above all, witness the numberless presents made to him by Marie Louise. But, like all true amateurs, he much preferred buying to receiving.

One morning the Emperor noticed a stick in Corvisart's hand. "What have you got in your hand?" said he. "It is my cane,

NAPOLEON AND CORVISART.

Sire." "It is very ugly; it is not pretty. How can a man like you carry such an ugly stick as that?" "Sire, that cane cost me a great deal of money, although I got it very cheap." "Tell me, Corvisart! what did it cost?" "Fifteen hundred francs, Sire; it is not dear." "*Ah! mon Dieu!* Fifteen hundred francs! Show me that ugly stick." The Emperor took the cane, examined it in detail, and discovered on the handle a little gilt medallion of Jean Jacques Rousseau. "Tell me, Corvisart, it is the cane of Jean Jacques; where did you get it? No doubt one of your patients made you a present of it. Well, really, it is a delightful relic you have there." "Pardon me, Sire, I gave fifteen hundred francs for it." "Really, Corvisart, you have not paid enough for it, for he was a great man—that is to say, a great charlatan. Really, Corvisart, he was a great man of his kind; he did some good things." And he pulled Corvisart's ears, saying, "Corvisart, you want to ape Jean Jacques!" and laughed.

The chase was one of the passions of Corvisart, and when he started for it he never said where he was going, for fear that they should send after him; but he loved to hunt at his country house of La Garenne, or at Vésinet with Lannes, the son-in-law of his friend Guéhéneuc, shooting for its own sake in the company of gay companions. One morning, when the Emperor was going to shoot at Saint Germain, he said to his first physician, "I want you to come shooting with me; I want to see if you are a good shot." Corvisart excused himself, saying that he had not got his guns. The Emperor replied that he should have some of his. Corvisart answered that he could not use them because he was left-handed; and at last he only gave way to the formally expressed desire of Napoleon.

These are scenes taken from life, which give the tone of these conversations at the *petit lever*. We hear that voice, of such beautiful quality that however softly it speaks it goes to the very depth of the heart; that pronunciation which possesses, as says a contemporary, a character of accentuation so remarkable as to be unique; the scansion of the words, which makes them sing, gives them their full value, makes the long syllables ring with a resonance not to be forgotten. In his moments of gaiety there was no noisy laugh; no more than a slight change of voice, a moment of irony, with the merest passage of a smile in the eyes.

In the absence of Corvisart the Emperor chatted with his *valet-de-chambre*, took an interest in what was talked of in town, listened to the gossip, and amused himself with the tittle-tattle of the day. This was part of the duty of Constant, and afterwards of Marchand. His curiosity was insatiable. They were compelled to report to him all the trifling talk of the town, " even the doings and quarrels of valets."

While still talking he took a cup of tea or of orange-flower water, which the first *valet-de-chambre* handed to him on the silver-gilt salver from the great travelling-case. The silver-gilt cup also came from the travelling-case, and the Emperor made a point of not being served with other vessels. He sweetened the infusion himself, and if he detected the slightest bad taste in it, he rejected it at once, according to the advice which Corvisart had given him. It was the only precaution he took against poison.

Having put on red or green slippers, which he used till they were completely worn out, and which he could not bear to have renewed, he went generally into his bath-room, which was formerly the oratory of Anne of Austria, and afterwards, when the alterations of the apartment took place, a little room fitted up near to the bed-room. With him the warm bath amounted to a passion. He often remained in it a whole hour, continually turning on the hot-water tap, and raising the temperature to such a point that the room was entirely full of steam, so that they were obliged to open the door. If urgent despatches arrived, his private secretary read them to him, otherwise he rapidly analysed the contents of the newspapers to him. The bath, besides being agreeable to him, was also necessary. Napoleon, in fact, had been troubled since his infancy with an obstinate constipation. As early as 1797, in Italy, he had suffered from hæmorrhoids, of which in truth, as he wrote, he had radically cured himself by the application of three or four leeches; but at the same time he also felt the first attacks of a complaint which threatened to become more frequent and more painful as he advanced in age. On that account he remained longer and longer in the bath, in which at St. Helena he came to the point of passing his days, and even his nights.

On leaving the bath, he put on a waistcoat of flannel, a shirt similar to that which he wore at night (for his shirts of *demi-hollande* at sixty francs, and afterwards at forty-eight francs, a-piece, were all of the same pattern); then he put on his chamber costume, composed in summer of a pair of a sort of drawers with feet, and of a long coat or dressing-gown of white twilled dimity; in winter of drawers of stout twilled cotton with feet, and of a dressing-gown of white duffle. On his head he kept the bandana which he slept in, knotted over the forehead, the two corners of which hung down behind on his shoulders. In this costume he worked for a long time with his secretary, and began to dictate his letters, or even, if it was a case of urgency, he received one of the Ministers in the back cabinet.

During all this time the *valet-de-chambre* had got the dressing-room ready, and the keeper of the wardrobe, Charvet, had brought in the garments. Of the *valets-de-chambre* one is celebrated — Roustam the Mameluke. The Emperor accepted him in Egypt from the

Sheik El Becri, brought him to France, had him taught at Versailles by Boutet to understand the care of arms, and took him everywhere. Many of the general officers who made the Egyptian expedition had a Mameluke in their suite: for instance, Eugène, Murat, Bessières, and several others; but Roustam alone was popular. At every parade, in every procession, he was to be seen, dressed in astonishing costumes, loaded with embroidery, his head covered with a cap of blue or crimson velvet embroidered with gold and surmounted with an aigrette, galloping about on a horse in Oriental trappings, and making his sabre ring. For the coronation his two costumes, which Isabey designed, cost 9,000 francs. Roustam, who received 2,400 francs as Mameluke, had besides 2,400 francs as assistant *porte arquebuse*; and his gratuities were at least double his wages. After each campaign 3,000 francs; on new year's day, 3,000, 4,000, 6,000 francs; in the year XIII 500 livres' annuity; at Fontainebleau, in 1814, in addition to a lottery office, 50,000 francs. When he married, in 1806, the daughter of Douville, *valet-de-chambre* of the Empress, it was Napoleon who paid for his wedding dinner—1,341 francs. All this did not prevent the Mameluke, in 1814, from following his comrade Constant in his desertion. But who knows, as regards these valets, what influences moved them?

Roustam was not deficient in power of observation; we may judge this from his recollections, one of the most curious documents which have been published on the period of the Empire. He was brave, like his companions of the squadron of Mamelukes, in which he served until 1806, very alert in his duty, which consisted in following the Emperor everywhere in campaign, and, at the Tuileries or elsewhere, in sleeping in the room immediately outside that in which Napoleon slept. Every night a folding bed was prepared for him. As more cleanly, Duroc wished to fit him up a bed in a closet; but one night the Emperor, instead of knocking, came himself to look for his Mameluke, and not being able to find him at first, got into a rage. The original arrangements were then reverted to.

At first the duty of Roustam was much more complicated; it was he who at table waited on the First Consul; but when the pages came he waited no longer. Under the Consulate he always appeared with the staff, as is shown in the *Revue du Décadi*, in which Isabey has not failed to place his portrait. But that displeased the officers, and, in spite of the Emperor's orders to furnish him with a horse, every pretext was used to prevent him from mounting it. In short, little by little he was ranked only as a servant like the others; but it was impossible to deprive him of his prestige. Every stranger who came to Paris wanted to see him. One of them wrote in 1807: "Roustam has a good face, and a good-natured expression, which is seldom seen among his compatriots. His complexion is not very dark. He is big and fat." And he troubled himself about his country, and about his marriage "with a pretty Parisienne." At any rate, ever since his arrival in Paris, Roustam was accustomed to make a sensation wherever he went. In the year VIII, the 10th Brumaire, at the performance of *La Caravane*, his feelings were watched with a view of making an article for the *Moniteur*; they printed his strange remarks: they contrived to make a success for him. All the painters hastened to take his portrait, which was circulated by means of engraving by thousands of copies; and Mdlle. Hortense de Beauharnais profited by the circumstance that a fall from his horse had prevented him from following the First Consul to Marengo, to ask him for sittings, and to make a fine drawing of him to give to her schoolmistress. As the sittings were very tedious to Roustam, she even sang pretty songs to him to keep him awake. How was it possible for this great child not to be spoilt? At least, unlike Constant, he had only acted thoughtlessly, for in 1815, on the return from the Island of Elba, he was anxious to return to the service of the Emperor; but Napoleon replied to Marchand, who had consented to present his petition: "He is a rogue; put it in the fire, and never speak to me of him." So brisk a reply from him, who at that moment pardoned every thing and every one, shows deep feeling, and proves to what an extent he had trusted this man; what an affection—of a special kind, as for a dog—he had had for him.

As to the theatrical legends, which aimed at showing Roustam as a fierce man, a sort of executioner attached to the person of the Emperor, is it necessary to go into them?

General Bonaparte brought from Egypt a second Mameluke, named Ali, whom he gave to Madame Bonaparte. But this Ali, who was horribly ugly, was even more wicked, and drew his poignard on every occasion. Although Josephine was full of kindness towards him, he got on so badly with the whole household that it ended in his being sent to Fontainebleau as *garçon d'appartement*. To replace him, just before 1811, the Emperor took into his service Louis Étienne Saint-Denis, who was then, it seems, only thirteen or fourteen years of age, and who, although born at Versailles, was none the less called Ali as soon as he entered the household, and took the costume of a Mameluke. Saint-Denis, called Ali, from the first accompanied the Emperor on campaign. In 1814 he was shut up in Mayence, and as soon as he could rejoined his master in the Island of Elba. In 1815 he made the whole of the Waterloo campaign, embarked on the *Bellerophon*, and took part in all the long agony of St. Helena. His name is inscribed in the will.

We may well think that at the toilet his duty

amounted to very little. But it was not so with the three *valets-de-chambre*, Sénéchal, Pélard, and Hubert. Ségur has said of Hubert that he was the most distinguished on account of his education, his intelligence, his talents, and his character. He could draw in an intelligent manner, and we have a portrait of the Emperor by him which is a document of interest. Hubert, who with Pélard followed his master to the Island of Elba, re-entered his *chambre* in 1815. Sénéchal and Pélard had then been made stewards of castles.

It is necessary to show by figures how Napoleon treated all this little world. The wages of the *valets-de-chambre* (2,400 francs), in addition to livery at 1,200 francs, were increased by an allowance of 6 francs a day on campaign, with an addition of gratuities varying from 1,500 to 3,000 francs a head. If one of them married, the Emperor gave him 6,000 francs. It is true that, if not in Paris, at least on campaign, the calling was a hard one, and they ran risks.

The necessity of making provision for services somewhat scattered all over Europe, at all the places which the Emperor might be called on to visit, explains the number of *valets-de-chambre* attached to his toilet, to whom must still be added Charvet, the keeper of the wardrobe, and three valets of the wardrobe, who also took their turns in going on campaign (one of them, Clément, died on the return from Russia), and some *garçons d'appartement*. Napoleon, from the first days of his success, showed a lordly desire to be waited on. In Egypt he had three *valets-de-chambre*. "Valets are the men for him," said Constant; and this saying represents him to the life.

He could not do with less than two to shave him. Very few men at that time shaved themselves, and that the Emperor should have learned to shave himself was a matter of astonishment. Madame de Rémusat attempts to give the credit of it to M. de Rémusat, master of the wardrobe. "He had seen," said she, "the agitation, not to say the actual anxiety, which Bonaparte experienced as long as this operation performed by a barber lasted." Constant relates more simply that after Ambart left, Hébert, who succeeded him, being exceedingly nervous and timid, could never make up his mind to shave the Emperor; that this duty then devolved on him (Constant); that the necessity of having recourse day after day to the same *valet-de-chambre* entailed on Napoleon a continual restraint (for he *never* submitted himself to a professional barber—apart from etiquette, prudence forbade it); that he wished to free himself from it, and after numerous unfortunate attempts he succeeded.

Let us not be astonished; the habit of shaving oneself is very recent. In the eighteenth century the perruquier played so important a part in life, a part so necessary, that it was natural to devolve on him this operation, which counted as a trifle among his other duties. It was only when the attempt was made to simplify masculine existence by divesting it of the fripperies of costume and toilet, by doing away with wigs, with powder, and with the various refinements of dressing the hair, by a uniformity of dress which reduced it to simple clothes instead of a personal adornment, and by abandoning perfumes and jewellery, that people came also to wish to free themselves from the barber, as afterwards they freed themselves from the hairdresser. But in the time of Napoleon and even in the generation which succeeded him, the men who shaved themselves were infinitely rare. They got the character of eccentricity, and did not fail to be considered remarkable. No doubt the barber-surgeons, to keep their clients together, had fostered the notion that this operation was one of singular delicacy and required infinite care; for, even if any one determined on doing it himself, he none the less approached it with a certain apprehension, and with the Emperor especially the ceremony was very elaborate.

Constant presented the basin and the soap; Roustam held the large mirror of the travelling case on the side of the light. The Emperor, in a flannel waistcoat, flooded one side of his face with lather, which he splashed all round him; then he wiped himself, took a razor with a handle of mother-of-pearl inlaid with gold, which had been previously dipped in hot water, and began to shave himself *from above downwards*, which at first was the cause of several accidents, for it seems it is a doctrine with barbers that shaving should be performed *from below upwards*.

It has been said that Napoleon used only English razors, which he had bought for him in Birmingham, and which cost two guineas the

SHAVING.

pair. On several occasions, however, his goldsmith, Biennais, furnished, for his travelling-cases, razors with pearl handles; but certain boxes for six and twelve razors perhaps contained English razors. As to the shaving soap, the cakes of soap scented with sweet herbs, or with orange, which Gervais-Chardin supplied, seem to have been entirely French.

As soon as the Emperor had shaved one side of his face every one turned round. Roustam, with his mirror, passed from right to left, or from left to right, following the light; and the operation continued. The Emperor, before finishing, asked every one if he was well shaved. Cheerful and fond of a joke, he commonly pulled the ears of his *valets-de-chambre* if he discovered that a hair had escaped him. His beard was thick, rather hard, and appears to have varied in colour; but this is supposition rather than a matter of certainty. Never, at any period of his life, except during his very last days at St. Helena, did he miss being shaved; a beard of a week's growth was a phenomenon with him. From the few hairs which have been seen, preserved in collections, no decision can be formed as to their colour.

After he had shaved, the Emperor washed his hands with almond paste and rose or Windsor soap; he washed his face with small and very fine sponges, and frequently dipped his head into a silver basin, which from its size might have been taken for a small copper. Such was the washing-stand of fifteen inches diameter which was taken from the Élysée to St. Helena in 1815. Having washed his face and hands, he picked his teeth very carefully with a boxwood toothpick, and then brushed them for some time with a brush dipped in opiate; went over them again with fine tooth-powder, and rinsed his mouth with a mixture of brandy and fresh water. Lastly, he scraped his tongue with a scraper of silver, of silver-gilt, or of tortoiseshell. It was to these minute precautions that he attributed the perfect preservation of all his teeth, which were beautiful, strong, and regular. During the whole of his reign he never appears to have had recourse, except for scaling, to Dubois, his surgeon-dentist, borne on the lists for six thousand francs, and the recipient of a gold travelling-case, the instruments in which were for the exclusive use of the Emperor.

The other toilet instruments which Napoleon

used also came exclusively out of his travelling-cases, which Biennais, at the sign of the Singe Violet, No. 283, Rue Saint-Honoré, supplied. In addition to the great cases containing a complete collection of all the necessaries for work, for the toilet, and for meals, such as the one which he bequeathed to his son, and which was given to the city of Paris by General Bertrand—such, again, as the great case bought on his return from Spain in January 1809—he had dressing-cases of a much more moderate size and weight; cases for packing, which would go into a holster, and of which he made use on campaign when separated from the baggage.

The care which he took of his person, his over-scrupulous cleanliness, the desire which he displayed for large quantities of water to wash in, accorded little with the habits of his time. Madame de Rémusat declares that "he had no idea whatever of the decency which good education generally implants in every well brought up person." There is no doubt that he felt no embarrassment in letting himself be seen undressed, nor in making his toilet in the presence of his intimate servants, or even, if necessary, before the whole army, as he did, for example, at the Island of Lobau ; but he never for a moment had the idea that there was anything indecent in it. The custom of camps, where the general is always visible to his *aides-de-camp* in whatever costume he happens to be, had no doubt disposed him to look on such modesty as hypocrisy. Perhaps also the Greek blood of the Kalomeroi, his ancestors, was not opposed to that feeling of *ease*—if one may say so—*in nudity*, which is found in him, as in several of his race. The nude in sculpture, in painting, in nature, did not shock them ; it appeared antique.

Having thus washed, the Emperor, with very great carefulness, trimmed his nails with scissors, which he insisted on having very sharp and accurate. He had beautiful hands, was aware of it, and took care of them in consequence. If the scissors did not cut to his fancy he broke them on the marble. On this account Biennais supplied them by the dozen. The profession of " manicure " had quite recently been invented by some of those women who had been ruined by the Revolution ; but Napoleon never employed a manicure, while for chiropodist he had a certain Tobias Koenig, a German Jew, who had obtained permission to wear a sword, and a coat embroidered like those of the *valets-de-chambre.* Koenig, who was a very little man, and kept much of his German accent, came once a fortnight to the toilet. Napoleon had seldom any necessity for his services, but he amused himself by asking him a string of questions about his clients, and for that Koenig was paid two thousand four hundred francs.

Another artist came once a week. This was Duplan, hairdresser to Their Majesties; "the only man who knew how to cut the hair," said the Emperor; "the only man who knew how to dress the hair," said Joséphine. She had so thoroughly convinced Napoleon of his talents that after the divorce nothing would do but that Duplan should be attached exclusively to the new Empress. He was paid 4,000 francs wages on the list of the household, 6,000 francs allowance from the privy purse of Marie Louise, 6,000 francs (afterwards 12,000) allowance from the Emperor's privy purse, and 1,166 francs a month from the treasury of the theatres. It became necessary to do this to induce him to give up his private connection, for Joséphine allowed him to dress hair for his general customers, which Napoleon expressly forbade when he placed him at the service of Marie Louise. Consequently, in spite of his salary of 40,000 francs, Duplan made out that he lost by the arrangement, and did not hesitate to ask for gratuities, some of which reached to 12,000 francs. He, too, succeeded in amusing the Emperor by telling him the gossip of the day. It stood him in good stead; he made his fortune, and his son, under the Second Empire, was an influential deputy.

The Emperor's hair was not black but auburn. For the exact colour we must without doubt not depend upon those specimens which, having been preserved under glass, have possibly lost their colour by exposure to light; but there are specimens which have been carefully wrapped up, and have remained so since the time they were taken from his head. These tend almost to a dark flaxen, in keeping with the blue—rather deep blue—eyes.

It was only at the end of the Consulate that he made up his mind to wear his hair quite short at the neck, and we may suppose that the reason must have been the very early baldness which is already foreshadowed in Gérard's fine portrait of 1803. In Italy he wore his hair quite long, flowing over his temples, a few locks only tied up into a pigtail with a ribbon. The whole of his head was at that time slightly powdered. On coming back from Italy he gave up powder at Joséphine's request; but he kept his hair long during the passage from Toulon to Alexandria. At Cairo, possibly even at the battle of the Pyramids, his hair was shorter. The hair on the temples has disappeared—all that light and floating veil which surrounded his face—and except at the back his hair is cut pretty close; but not so much as might be fancied—witness a series of busts executed on his return to France, from nature, which still show some long locks falling over the forehead, covering three-quarters of the ears, and encroaching considerably on the collar. At the same time the First Consul allowed his whiskers to grow as far as a third of the cheeks, which went down lower than the lobe of the ear, and appear to be pretty thick. These whiskers disappeared at the same time that the hair became shorter at the back; but it was only quite at the end of the Consulate that Bonaparte became "*le Tondu*" (the shorn), as the soldiers called him. Gradually from that time the forehead became bare; so much so that in some of the unflattered sketches of the end of the Empire, we see that he brings the hair forward, and that the long lock which gives so lively a character to his face comes from a distance.

Having attended to his nails, Napoleon took off his flannel jacket, had some *eau-de-Cologne* poured on his head, and with a stiff brush himself brushed his chest and arms. The *valet-de-chambre* afterwards scrubbed his back and shoulders with the brush, and then applied friction to the whole of his body, pouring on it phials full of *eau-de-Cologne*. This habit of rubbing, which Napoleon had, as he said, brought from the East, and to which he partly attributed his health, seemed to him most important. They were not allowed to do it gently. "Harder," said he to the *valet-de-chambre*; "harder! as though you were rubbing an ass!"

Like the baths, the rubbing and the brush were calculated in his case to keep the skin in such a condition as to be always able to perform its functions. "In his case," said one of his physicians, "as soon as the tissue of the skin became thickened by any cause, the commencement of irritation with more or less serious results showed itself, and the cough and other symptoms declared themselves violently." These symptoms yielded to the re-establishment of the action of the skin. The violent perspirations which he brought on, partly by baths of great duration, partly by means of a great excess of covering on his bed, warmed till it was scarcely bearable, partly by rides on horseback of sixty kilomètres, had the same object. After great fatigues he condemned himself, always with the same object, to twenty-four hours of absolute rest. Lastly, his temperament manifested a very singular peculiarity recurring periodically, which had an ascertained influence on his health, the cessation of which, at St. Helena, coincided with the aggravation of his unhealthy state. "I shall be cured if I perspire, and if the wounds which I have on my thigh re-open," said he on January 22nd, 1821, three months before his death; but "nature no longer answered to the promptings of his will."

Having been thus bathed, washed, and

rubbed, the Emperor dressed himself. He put on his flannel waistcoat, over which, after 1808, he wore on campaign, suspended by a black cord, a little heart of black satin of the size of a large hazel-nut. Under the silken envelope was another envelope of skin, in which was enclosed poison prepared according to the formula which was given by Cabanis to Condorcet, and which appeared to be infallible. Later, in 1812, the Emperor substituted for this poison another prepared by Yvan, according to a different formula, and this poison played him false in 1814; but at the time of his departure for Spain he took precautions so as not to fall alive into the hands of the enemies of France. If in 1815, after Waterloo, although in possession of a means of death, the effect of which he knew, and which he carried about constantly on his person in a bag formed in his braces, he did not choose to make use of it, it was because he thought it well that his destinies should be fulfilled, and that he might furnish with this prodigious example of human vicissitudes the sole revenge which his martyrdom and death could procure for conquered France against victorious England.

Then came the shirt. Afterwards Constant put on his feet very light merino socks, over which he drew stockings of white silk, kept up by elastic garters; he handed to him a pair of drawers of very fine linen, or twilled cotton, and a pair of knee-breeches of white kerseymere, fastened at the knee with a small gold buckle. At times when, instead of shoes with gold buckles, Napoleon was going to put on soft riding boots, he wore very tight pantaloons of white kerseymere or of knitted cotton. The knee-breeches or pantaloons were held up with elastic braces.

It was Chevalier, his tailor, who supplied the flannel waistcoats at 40 francs each; his shirts came from the great linendrapers Mdes. Lolive, de Beuvry & Co., Rue Neuve-des-Petits-Champs, who also supplied the stocks of black twill, at 8 francs apiece. The silk stockings, from Panier's, cost 18 francs the pair; but Napoleon complained of it. "Why dearer for me than for any one else?" said he. "I don't understand that. Ought I to be robbed?" His shoes, as well as his boots, were very easy, a centimètre longer than his foot, which measured exactly 26 centimètres, half a centimètre broader at the middle of the sole, which measured 7 centimètres. Further, the shoes with gold buckles, which Jacques, Rue Montmartre, supplied, were lined with silk, and care was taken to have them worn into shape for three days by a young man of the wardrobe named Joseph Linden, who had exactly the same foot as the Emperor. The shoes cost generally 15 francs a pair. Sometimes, but very rarely, and no doubt on campaign, Napoleon appears to have worn clogs over his shoes. For hunting, as he always did when he rode on horseback, he put on over his silk stockings riding boots with linings either of morocco or of silk plush, which received every day a fresh dressing. He was thus able to change them for shoes without having to change his stockings. These boots, which cost 80 francs the pair, were fitted with little silver spurs, scarcely more than a centimètre in length, some of which were very much worn out. Napoleon had twelve pairs, and the *valets-de-chambre* knew on what occasions such or such a pair had been worn; thus, the spurs of the campaign of Dresden and of the campaign of France, which Napoleon offered to Las

Cosas saying, "Take them, *mon cher*, I used them at Champaubert."

Having put on his shoes and a very thin cravat of muslin, and over it a stiff stock of black silk, very high and broad, and with a flap in front, Napoleon put on a round waistcoat of white kerseymere; a waistcoat coming lower down than the waistcoats of to-day. This waistcoat was reckoned, with the knee-breeches, at 85 francs by the usual tailor Chevalier, at 64 francs by Lejeune, who in 1815 replaced Chevalier. The Emperor changed his waistcoat and knee-breeches every morning, only wearing them when clean, and having them washed only three or four times. Careful as he was of his person, he was very little so of his clothes. He wiped his pen on his breeches, or he splashed the ink about by tossing his pen on his writing table. This did not make him change them during the day, any more than his silk stockings, although he had the habit of rubbing one leg with the heel of the shoe of the other foot when it itched. The renewing of the waistcoats and knee-breeches was a serious matter. Forty-eight were to be supplied yearly, and they ought to have lasted three years, but there was always a deficiency. In 1811, on going through the wardrobe, there were only seventy-four instead of one hundred and forty-four; the others must have been put aside.

Over his waistcoat he buckled on his swordbelt. The shape of this belt changed at different times. The Emperor tried a belt with buckles in the form of shields, ornamented with eagles' heads, charged with the initial letter N, and each one furnished with an S hook in the form of a serpent; he had belts of purple silk, belts of black leather, belts of deerskin lined with gold; he even used light crossbelts worn over his shirt and under his waistcoat, in which the sword was slipped into a simple loop of white leather. But in the general way his sword belt, which he took off in his cabinet, was worn over or under the waistcoat.

Napoleon had only two swords in constant use, both with gold hilts, with sheaths of tortoiseshell mounted in gold. On the hilt of one, in the middle, was represented an Iron Crown surrounded with a wreath of laurel, and on each side the heads of Minerva and Hercules in medallions enriched with arabesques. The pommel terminated with a helmet and was formed of an owl; the bow, ornamented with eagles and bees, was finished off with a small antique lion's head; the guard, consisting of a reversed shell, was chased with a shield charged with an eagle grasping thunderbolts; on the edge of the shield were placed sixteen bees, as many as there were cohorts in the Legion of Honour; the blade of cast steel was incrusted with ornament. Biennais supplied this sword, which cost 5,700 francs.

One might be tempted to suppose that the Emperor had more than two swords in general use; but only two are to be found in the different inventories. No doubt he had swords of ceremony, but in very small number. In 1811 he possessed in all four swords: the two in general use, a sword of French pattern of silver gilt, and a sword with a straight blade and an ivory hilt. The sword which the Emperor wore at Austerlitz, that which after that day he had almost constantly at his side, which he bequeathed to his son and which General Bathier, who had charge of it, offered to King Louis Philippe, is preserved in the *cella* of the tomb at the Invalides.

On his waistcoat Napoleon wore the *grand cordon* of the Legion of Honour; it was only on occasions of state that he wore it upon his coat.

Finally, the Emperor was handed his coat, generally the coat of the *chasseur à cheval* of his guard; on Sundays, and for ceremonies when he did not put on state dress, the coat of the foot grenadiers. The grenadiers' coat was of royal blue cloth; the collar blue, without piping; the lapels white, cut square, without piping; the cuffs scarlet, without piping; the flaps white, with three points; the lining scarlet, without piping, turned back, caught up and decorated with four grenades embroidered with gold on white cloth; the cut of the pocket longways, marked by an edging of scarlet; the gilt buttons bore an eagle crowned. The coat of the *chasseurs à cheval* was of green cloth, lapels pointed, lining of the same cloth; collars and cuffs (pointed) red; gussets in the folds, green, piped with red; facings ornamented with hunting-horns embroidered in gold; hussar buttons bearing an eagle crowned. Certain coats—among others the one at the museum at Sens—have the buttons round and plain.

It was in Vendémiaire, year IX, that the First Consul began to wear these uniforms. At Morfontaine, at the house of Joseph Bonaparte, he saw a coat folded up on an armchair. He took it up and unfolded it; it was the coat of a colonel of the consular guard. " I should like to try it," said he, and undressing, he put it on. "It is a very handsome coat," said he, looking at himself in the glass. "I do not know a finer, unless it is my coat of officer of artillery." From that moment he adopted it for common use—for on ceremonial occasions he put on the coat of a general or consul —and during the Empire he wore no other. It was perhaps in imitation of Frederic II., who never wore anything but military uniform, and by preference that of his foot guards. This had become traditional among those sovereigns who were his admirers. In 1815 Napoleon occasionally put on the uniform of the national guard, but he never wore it during the Consulate, although it has been asserted; the resemblance between the two coats of the national guard and the foot grenadiers may have caused the confusion.

Light and somewhat small epaulettes, with

the body quite plain, the edge narrow and with bullion fringe, were all passed through the loop of the coat, which, as regards decorations, was embellished only with the badge of the grand eagle of the Legion, embroidered in silver, and with the two decorations of the Legion of Honour and of the Iron Crown. The badge of the Legion which the Emperor wore was, up to the time of Austerlitz, the decoration in silver of a legionary, *not surmounted with the crown*, which was not added till April 1806. After Austerlitz, he assumed the gold eagle of an officer, and kept it up to his death. From June 5th, 1805, he always wore at the same time as the Legion of Honour, the gold decoration of his order of the Iron Crown ; it was the Lombard crown, ornamented with a medallion of the crowned profile of the founder, surmounted with an eagle, and suspended to an orange ribbon with green edging. He never wore the insignia of the order of the Three Fleeces, founded by him August 15th, 1809, the decoration of which was only projected ; and only two or three portraits are known in which he is represented with the cordon or the star of the order of the Réunion, instituted

October 18th, 1811. Nevertheless, in certain clusters (*jeux*) of decorations which belonged to him, the blue ribbon of the Réunion is found attached to the same bar as those of the Iron Crown and the Legion. It is probable that he wore it at least during his voyage of 1811 in the United Provinces, for the two portraits mentioned are by Dutch painters.

The coat of the "*chasseur à cheval*" cost 200 or 210 francs; the pair of epaulettes 148 francs; the badge of the legion 62 francs. The grenadier coat, which was dearer, amounted to 240 or 250 francs. The tailor Chevalier had a constant tendency to raise his prices. Thus, in 1813 we find another tailor, Lejeune, sending in grenadiers' coats, with epaulettes and badge, at 340 francs, and chasseurs' coats, complete, at 330 francs. This was the result of the administration of M. de Turenne, the new master of the wardrobe.

The Emperor had, in fact, on August 19th, 1811, given M. de Rémusat to understand that "he had nothing more to do with his wardrobe." It was most unseemly that tradesmen should come to him to demand payment of their bills. "While I was at Saint-Cloud," said he, " in my *calèche*, with the Empress at my side, and in the midst of an immense concourse of people, I found myself called upon all of a sudden in the Eastern fashion, as if I had been the sultan going to mosque, by a man who had worked for my person and claimed a considerable sum, the payment of which had been refused him for a long time."

Whether by bad management or by malversation, M. de Rémusat had allowed debts to accumulate, and that without keeping up the wardrobe as it should have been. If it was negligence it was the more culpable, for he owed his position, and that of his wife, entirely to the Emperor. Raised by him from obscurity, almost from misery ; placed at first among the servants of the Consul, then elevated to the dignity of Chamberlain, and even of First Chamberlain ; invested with the title of Count, and tacitly authorised to use a particle to which he had no right whatever ; loaded with those pecuniary benefits which are honourable to the man who remains faithful, and dishonourable to him who betrays his trust (among others a gratuity of 200,000 francs on the Emperor's order, dated Messidor 28, year XII), he was not one of those men whose too vast brain refuses to bring itself to bear on the every-day arrangements of a household; and he had proved that, if he was prodigal when his master was concerned, he was as niggardly as possible when it was a question of his own purse. M. and Madame Rémusat, in addition to their salaries for different offices, salaries amounting to 42,000 francs without perquisites, presents, privileges of the Directorship of the Theatres, and the rest, received in November 1807, for housekeeping and the reception of strangers, an allowance from the secret funds at first of 2,000 francs a month, and then, almost immediately, of 5,000. They received the whole of that sum in 1807 and 1808, which did not prevent them in October 1808 " from seriously thinking about receiving more people and fulfilling the intentions of the master." Seeing what use was made of his generosity, Napoleon, by way of warning to them, reduced the gratuity to 36,000 francs in 1809, and to 24,000 in 1810. It is true that the First Chamberlain and his wife might, from 1808, have been caught in the very act of conspiracy, and that after that time their opposition was increased. In 1811 was discovered the affair of the deficiency of 16,000 francs in the toilet, and the Emperor, while leaving M. Rémusat his place as First Chamberlain, withdrew his title of Master of the Wardrobe.

In order to justify her husband, Madame de Rémusat alleges that the 40,000 francs which, said she, were borne on the budget for the Emperor's toilet, could not possibly suffice. The amount which Madame de Rémusat mentions here is false. From the year XI to 1814 the toilet stood on the budget for 20,000 francs only; and from the moment when the wardrobe was administered by another than M. de Rémusat this amount was amply sufficient. This other person, M. le Comte de Turenne d'Aynac, possessed at the same time a real devotion to the person of the Emperor, as well as qualities which were entirely absent in his predecessor—order and economy in his service. Besides this, he was brave, as he had proved in the campaigns which he had gone through as an orderly officer; he was clever and well informed, and his stories amused the Emperor, who had nicknamed him, on account of his Anglomania, "Milord Kinsester." In addition to this, his duty as Master of the Wardrobe had been greatly simplified by Napoleon, who, having settled up the arrears, had had drawn up, in accordance with current prices, a detailed regulation of his requirements, with a complete inventory; he then settled how long the articles were to last, the giving of orders, and the retrenchments which were to be made, as he would have done in the case of one of his regiments.

When the Emperor had completed his toilet and prepared to leave his apartment, he took his hat, which the first valet handed to him, in his left hand. This hat, of black beaver, without border or lace, ornamented only with a small tricoloured cockade attached to a loop of black silk, was supplied by Poupard & Co., Palais du Tribunal, and cost 60 francs. Four were to be bought yearly, and each was to last three years. It was broad, of a comparatively soft beaver, and the crown was lined with quilted satin. In spite of this, it had still to be stretched before the Emperor, whose head was extremely sensitive, could wear it. This head-dress must have been singularly inconvenient, for when it had been exposed for a long time to the rain the beaver got soaked, and the flaps before and behind fell on his face and shoulders; but yet Napoleon was constant to it. It was his special distinction, and every one knew him by it.

It was only about the year 1802 that he adopted it, at the time when Isabey painted his portrait, on foot, at Malmaison. As long as the Consulate lasted no doubt he used it only on campaign and in private. On state occasions he had an embroidered hat, without plume. During the Empire he had a sort of leaning for a brass helmet, gilt. One, at least, was to be found in his wardrobe. In private clothes he wore a round hat; but it may be affirmed that he only wore private clothes on very rare occasions, for expeditions *incognito*. Thus, at the Tuileries he had no other hat than his *petit chapeau*; but, on the other hand, he always had it either in his hand or on his head whenever he went from one room to another. He took it by the front flap, and often waved it about in conversation. When he was angry, or wished to appear so, he threw it on the ground and kicked it with his foot.

After his hat the Emperor received from his *valet-de-chambre* a handkerchief on which some *eau-de-Cologne* was poured, which he placed to his lips, then to his forehead, and passed lightly over his temples. This handkerchief was of very fine lawn, marked, like all the linen supplied by Mdlles. Lolive & de Beuvry, with a crowned N. A few had printed borders of different colours. They cost invariably 12 francs each. Napoleon then took an eyeglass, a bonbonnière in which was liquorice mixed with aniseed, and a snuff-box. He never left his room till he had stowed away these different things in the pockets of his uniform. This habit was so well known to those around him that, at table, if he felt about fruitlessly in one of his pockets without finding what he wanted, the *maître d'hôtel* rushed off and at once brought back the desired article. "Why, Dunan," said the Emperor to him one day, "you must be a sorcerer always to know what I have forgotten!" "Sire," replied Dunan, "I have noticed that your Majesty always has his pocket-handkerchief in the right pocket, and his snuff-box in the left pocket."

The pocket eyeglasses, which were supplied by Lerebours, the celebrated optician of the Place du Pont-neuf, measured 18 to 21 lines, cost from 180 to 220 francs, and were usually of silver gilt. Although Napoleon was infinitely less short-sighted than his brothers Lucien and Jerome, he still had short sight, and had the constant habit, not only on campaign, but at Paris, of using an eyeglass or a binocular.

The bonbonnières were little round boxes of crystal or tortoiseshell, mounted in gold, some with a portrait, that of Madame Mère or of Queen Caroline. The liquorice was cut, or rather broken up, into extremely small pieces, so as simply to perfume the mouth and to melt at once without blackening the saliva. It was the only indulgence he allowed himself, and this was a perfume.

As to his snuff-boxes, Napoleon had them of all kinds, which were presented to him by the Pope, the Sultan, the Empresses Joséphine and Marie Louise, his mother, his sisters-in-law Catherine and Julie, and his sister Caroline. Some of those in the wardrobe dated from the earliest times of the Consulate, for he preserved small objects of this kind to which any recollection or association was attached. The snuff-box which he carried in Italy will be remembered, the lid of which was adorned with a portrait of his Joséphine, as well as the superstitious fear he experienced when he broke the glass of it. In Messidor, year IV, while still in Italy, he lost his snuff-box and at once wrote to Joséphine: "I beg you to choose rather a flat one for me, and to have something pretty inscribed on the top with your hair."

Throughout his life he never made use of sumptuous snuff-boxes studded with diamonds, cut out of rare stones, or carved at great expense; those which he preferred were oval snuff-boxes, narrow, with hinges, of tortoise-shell or even of wood, lined with gold and ornamented with cameos or antique coins. For example, an oval snuff-box, long, of tortoise-shell lined with gold, ornamented with four silver medals representing Regulus, Sylla, Pompey, and Julius Cæsar; an oval snuff-box, of tortoiseshell, lined with gold with a medallion painted by Isabey, representing the King of Rome; another with the portrait of Marie Louise, which was sent to him from Vienna at the time of the marriage,—were in common use. This idea of the medals is not a mere chance; it would seem that he wished to have his models, the great leaders of nations, constantly before his eyes: Alexander, Peter the Great and Charles XII, Charles V and Francis I, Frederic II, Augustus, Cæsar, and Timoleon; as well as the founders of dynasties, Demetrius Poliorcetes, Antiochus, Mithridates, Phraates II, and Constantine.

Oval snuff-boxes had the advantage that he could open them with one hand and without loss of time, as with round or square ones.

The snuff was ground very coarsely, composed of several sorts mixed, and supplied at the price of 3 francs to 3 francs 50 centimes a pound by Ancest or Robillard. It was kept in great pots of glazed stoneware, or in locked boxes of which the first valet alone had the key. Precautions were taken since the time when at La Malmaison the Consul found on a piece of furniture within his reach a snuff-box completely like his own, filled with poisoned snuff. After that no one but Constant had anything to do with his snuff.

One evening, at the moment when the Emperor was leaving table, a chamberlain noticed that the snuff-box was empty and hastened to have it filled. The Emperor took it, opened it, and threw the contents into the fire and made a sign to his *maître d'hôtel* to give him some snuff. This was not mistrust, but a way of pointing out that each person in his household had his own duty, and that officious attentions did not please him.

Napoleon consumed a great deal of snuff, and yet he took very little; but he took large pinches, which he passed under his nose without drawing them in, and then dropped at once. He often passed his open snuff-box backwards and forwards under his nose. His pocket-handkerchiefs were, so to speak, never soiled. It is somewhat in the same manner that he tried smoking. Not taking the pinch of snuff, but contenting himself with smelling it, so he also affected to smoke tobacco without inhaling, and rejecting it; or rather, he simply took a lighted Oriental pipe, put the amber mouthpiece between his lips, and when the smoke came out he began to cough and to spit, saying, "Pouah! Pouah! Take away this nasty thing!" And from that time he never tried again. The pipesticks of jasmine wood, with mouthpieces of amber set with precious stones, which he brought from Egypt, and which he showed to Moreau, Rue de la Victoire, a few days after Brumaire, remained, however, in the wardrobe, where they were found in August 1811.

It does not appear that the Emperor habitually carried a watch. If by chance he carried one, he took but little care of it, and in undressing he sent his watch flying like everything else that he had about him; if he happened to get in a passion, or to wish to simulate it, he threw his watch on the floor with violence, as he did with his hat; but the watch would not stand such treatment, therefore repairs were very frequent.

The watches which the Emperor had in his wardrobe, which he might have used, were repeaters, without ornament or initial, simply in a gold case, with glass over the face. Two were of silver, striking. They had been supplied by Lépine, Bréguet, and Magnier. Some had belonged to him ever since the Italian campaign. This was the case with the one he gave to the Grand Marshal at St. Helena with the remark: " Take it, Bertrand! it struck two o'clock at night at Rivoli when I gave Joubert orders to attack!"

As to money, Napoleon never took any with him. If he went out and wanted to give some trifling alms, he addressed himself to the *aide-de-camp*, to the equerry, or to the chamberlain on duty; in fact, to the first person who came to hand.

Indoors, he had in a drawer of his table rouleaus of gold for trifling assistance; if it was a question of a large sum he scrawled a draft on the treasurer-general or gave orders to the secretary to pay it from the petty cash.

At nine o'clock punctually, the toilet being complete, the official day began.

IV.

THE MORNING LEVÉE.

A FEW moments before nine o'clock there was a scratching at the door. It was the chamberlain of the day, in a coat of scarlet silk, embroidered with silver, with white waistcoat and knee-breeches, wearing on the right-hand pocket of his coat a large knot of green silk ribbon, with stripes and tassels of gold, to which was attached a key without any bit, the bow of which exhibited an escutcheon with the letter N, surmounted with a crowned eagle. This chamberlain, like all the officers on duty, whether civil or military, was always in uniform. The Emperor would not have tolerated—still less would he have ordered—that under pretext of convenience the persons attached to his household should divest themselves of their marks of office and appear in private dress. On the other hand, from the year 1807, any one who was not on duty, but who was invited to any festivity, was expected to present himself in a silk or velvet suit *à la française*. It was one of the means of advancing the manufactures of Lyons.

The Chamberlain then, who had a room at the Tuileries, and was able to dress himself there, had, since the morning, satisfied himself that the ushers and the *valets-de-chambre* of the *appartement* had done their duties, and that everything was in its place, and all the men at their posts. At the desired hour he came to the *salon de service*, and, having crossed the second *salon*, scratched at the door of the bedroom. A *valet-de-chambre* of the *appàrtement*, after having taken the Emperor's orders, ushered him in, and handed to him the list of the persons who attended the *levée*. Then, recrossing the *salon*, each door of which was kept by two ushers in a French coat of green cloth, embroidered with gold on the collar and on the facings, with red waistcoat and black knee-breeches, he returned to the *salon de service*, into which, by right of their privilege, the grand officers of the crown and the officers of the household whose day of attendance it was had entered.

These consisted of the Grand Chamberlain, whose uniform differed from that of the Chamberlain only in the richness of its embroidery, and his insignia of office only in the dimensions of his key; and with him came the Second Chamberlain, who was entrusted with the service of the state apartments. Then came the Grand Equerry, and the Equerry in a coat of bright blue, the Grand Master and the Master of the Ceremonies in violet. The Grand Master had a key similar to that of the Grand Chamberlain. The Grand Huntsman and the Lieutenant of the Hunt in green; the Prefect of the Palace (the Grand *Maréchal* having assisted at the toilet) in purple; the Grand Almoner and the Almoner of the day in cassocks, according to their ecclesiastical rank; then the *Intendant Général* and the Treasurer of the Crown; lastly, the colonel-general on duty, in the uniform of the corps of which he was in command; grenadiers or *chasseurs à pied*, chasseurs or artillery, with an aiguillette, the distinctive sign of the Guard, which also was worn by *aides-de-camp* on their uniforms of general or colonel.

At nine o'clock precisely the Emperor came

out of his private apartment. If he was ready earlier, he waited for the clock to strike before having the doors opened. He entered his *salon* at the same time as the household on duty, introduced by the chamberlain of the day. Unless under exceptional circumstances, or because Napoleon wished, from motives of policy, to allow some decision which he had come to, or some piece of news, to leak out—unless there was some necessity to set the absent right by addressing those who were present, or again, unless the Abbé de Pradt, his almoner, was at the *lever*, and Roman affairs required attention, the audience was short and almost silent, and the Emperor confined himself to giving the necessary orders very briefly.

If he took one of the grand officers aside, it was because he looked on him as the representative of some constituted body, or of a class of individuals. Thus, Ségur, the Grand Master of the Ceremonies, or Daru, the *Intendant Général*, both belonging to that second class of the Institut which represented the *Académie Française*, generally took this charge for the Academy; but they were not intended to take the very direct speeches of the Emperor as addressed to them individually. The effect which he aimed at was attained so soon as he knew that what passed at the *lever* would be talked about in Paris.

Except on such occasions, as far as regards those on duty, the *lever* consists rather in giving orders. Everything about it is military—in fact, cold and formal. No little stories are told, no good things repeated, no familiarity slips in, no kind expressions find a place. They are in attendance to receive orders and to hand in their reports. It is for this purpose that Napoleon understands their attendance at the *levers*, and expects them to be punctual. If any one arrives late, it is necessary to be prepared with some happy excuse, such as that attributed to Ségur in 1809: "It was impossible to get along the streets on account of the crowd of kings which I fell in with."

Those on duty having been dismissed with a slight bow, the chamberlain of the day introduced the *Grandes Entrées*. Those who enjoyed this privilege were the princes of the Imperial family and of the Empire, cardinals, the great officers of the Empire, the officers of the Empress's household, princes and princesses, with the presidents of the great bodies of the State, and the chief authorities of Paris. All these alighted at the bottom of the staircase of Flora, for their carriages entered the court of the palace, and they were almost the only carriages which did. They had been recognised on entry by the porter of the interior, Nivernais, passed up the stairs, and on the landing had been saluted with the halberd, according to their rank, by the porter of the apartment. They passed across the *salle des gardes*, that hall which Fontaine and Percier had just decorated, in which, on a ceiling of wonderful richness, is depicted Mars in his war chariot. On their approach, the pages, out of respect to them, rise from their benches, which were formerly covered with simple Utrecht velvet, but now with tapestry of the Savonnerie; then the doors of the *salon de service* having been opened on their approach by an usher, they settle down there to wait the Emperor's good pleasure.

There was nothing to do but to stand and exchange commonplaces, nothing even to please the eye. Except the furniture, chairs, and folding stools of wood gilt, covered with tapestry of Beauvais, with valances also of the same material—for tapestry also has its own degrees of rank, Gobelins for the Emperor, Beauvais for the household, Savonnerie for the pages—the whole decoration has remained the same as in the time of Louis XIV, with Maria Theresa, painted by Nocret, under the guise of Minerva, on the ceiling, and on the walls great ugly landscapes which have become almost black. The general effect is depressing. There is but little light in the apartments. It reminds one of the saying of Roederer to the First Consul, " This is melancholy, General!" "Yes," answered he, " like greatness."

Every one is in the costume of his station, the uniform of his rank or of his office, wearing his orders, in silk stockings and in shoes. The princes of the Imperial family, who are also kings, appear in the costume of French princes; Cambacérès does not fail to dress himself in the grand violet coat of arch-chancellor, Lebrun in the black coat of arch-treasurer; the vice-grand elector Talleyrand, when he sets aside his scarlet coat of grand chamberlain, wears a deep red coat; each wears a sword at his side, the hilt and pommel of which are formed of an eagle with outstretched wings, while the pearl handle is grooved and surmounted with a knob formed of two lions' heads. Ministers, senators, deputies, tribunes, prefects, and generals wear blue coats distinguished by the difference of the embroidery; the officers of the household of the Empress and of the princes are in the costumes of varied colours assigned to the service to which they belong. It is a wonderful picture, which, on certain occasions, is rendered even more brilliant by the presence of the princes of the Confederation of the Rhine in the uniform of their troops.

The *grandes entrées* are summoned, and, following the order of their rank, the chamberlain ushers the favoured ones into the *salon* of the Emperor, the six armchairs and the twelve chairs of which, of gilt wood, are covered with Gobelins tapestry, the curtains and the *portières* of the same manufacture, the furniture of gilt wood. The ceiling represents the triumph of Minerva, always represented by Maria Theresa. A circle is formed. The Emperor passes along it, and speaks to almost every one of the persons present, for he likes his *lever* to be numerous; he is not pleased when people stop away, and it is by their assiduity in attending this early ceremony that some of them succeed in escaping those suspicions which their conduct ought to arouse. Talleyrand, even in those days when he seems to be in the deepest disgrace, is the first to arrive, the last to leave. The first shock is over, and he has been neither arrested nor shot; he returns therefore every morning; the Emperor does not speak to him; people give him the cold shoulder, and leave an empty space around him; but he remains, and, obtruding his impassive countenance, waits, reckoning on the easy forgetfulness which Napoleon has for injuries. And he is justified in the end.

The Emperor, however, talks much more to those persons who are not constant attendants, to functionaries and general officers whom he has ordered the chamberlain on duty to summon to the *lever*, and from whom he wishes to get some information.

When the necessity arises of administering a rating to one of his Ministers, he is not in the habit of restraining himself because there is a crowd of people, and the lesson will therefore be less clear and less forcible; but now, as on every occasion, he only talks about business, and does not waste time on trifles. No conversation takes place which does not concern administration or politics, which touches on gallantry or concerns arrangements for amusement; questions which often disconcert by their precision and their minuteness, and require a clear answer, a simple figure, an explanation as short as possible; a skill in examination like that of a judge, the results of which his memory records more perfectly than any registrar; an attention always awake, which nothing wearies, and which travels over the Empire and over Europe with as much ease as it would over a district of a thousand souls, and which, absolutely without preparation, and without consulting a note, travels from Escaut to the Danube, from Napoléonville to Erfurt, always equally ready, equally imperious, without hesitation, without correcting himself, wresting human nature in this way in order to extract facts which help forward his designs. This is the spectacle which he offers every morning, which day by day forces more strongly on those who are present the habit of thinking no more themselves, so completely does he make it his business to think for all.

The *lever* does not last long, as might be supposed, for there is no idle talk; and if the Emperor has a wish to get to the bottom of a question, or if some great functionary has doubtful points to submit to him, it will be at a private audience.

These audiences begin as soon as the *lever* has been dismissed with a bow: they are given in the same room, for it cannot be too often repeated that no one enters the study. In the first place are those personages who, having the *grandes entrées*, have shown at the *lever* a wish to speak to the Emperor. Then come all those who have asked and obtained an audience. The chamberlain of the day has in his hands a list from which he does not depart, for the Emperor has an exact copy before him, and will allow of no alteration by favour; but there are fools—M. de Rémusat, for example. One day, at Saint-Cloud, Count Dubois, *Préfet* of the Police, stepping into his carriage in the court of the *château*, on coming away from an audience with the Emperor, heard himself called from the balcony by Napoleon, who had omitted an important order. Dubois returned in haste, but in the *salon de service* he found M. de Rémusat, the chamberlain of the day, who refused to let him go in. Dubois protested and explained; but M. de Rémusat would listen to nothing. He only knew his orders. During this time the Emperor began to be astonished, then got impatient, and finally opened the door and found Dubois in hot dispute with this refractory chamberlain. It is asserted that the Emperor made an offensive remark about the intellect of M. de Rémusat. Who knows if some other word would not have hit the mark better? The talk was all about Fouché, the lover of Madame de Rémusat, whom she had just reconciled with her other lover, M. de Talleyrand; and it was therefore quite natural that the First Chamberlain should try to avoid making orders given against his accomplice by the Emperor more stringent.

Except in the case of the Ministers and the functionaries whom he retained after the *lever*, it was seldom that in these morning audiences, all of which were very short, anything passed about general affairs. In most cases they are persons who wish to present some personal request; and the Emperor knows so far in advance what it will be about, that he seldom gives an audience except when he has made up his mind to grant the favour which will be asked. Sometimes, however, it pleases him to exhibit to all who happen to be present, his worst enemies in his ante-chambers in the position of suppliants, and then he makes them wait some time for their turn of favour; for it is a matter of concern to him that it should be generally known that if a certain conspirator has been pardoned, such a prisoner released, or such an exile recalled, at least the step has been the result of solicitation; and he is of opinion that the authenticated presence in his palace of a member of a family will oblige those allied to it to preserve a certain discretion in their designs.

It would astonish people much if a complete list were given of those of both sexes who obtained audiences, and, in consequence, favours. In addition to the princes of the House of Bourbon—and, again, there were some of them even who received important assistance and a regular allowance—most of the families of the ancient *noblesse* owe to the kindness of the Emperor

AN AUDIENCE.

alone the gracious gifts of landed estates which at the present day still form their fortune. Although some of these restitutions were justified by services rendered in war, the larger part were an encouragement for services at court, and all were solicited and obtained in this manner.

The Emperor received standing upright before the fireplace, in which till very late in the season a roaring fire was kept up; this he was always knocking with the heel of his shoes. His clear eyes, of a blue which changed colour, at times almost black, when he concentrated his attention, at other moments of steely grey, when seized with emotion or anger, so bright then that they seemed like molten metal, fastened attentively on the person who addressed him, whom he heard to the end. He then put some short questions, at times not over courteous if it was a woman. He had not learned the art of talking to ladies, and was not happy in his manner with them: some got angry and answered sharply. He bore them no grudge, and was amused at it. It was very unusual for a woman to leave his *salon* without carrying away with her, in addition to the favour which she had come to ask, some sharpness of feeling against him who had granted it to her. As to men, some are mentioned who, as the result of an audience, became devoted to him. They were rare.

The demands for money which were made to him were as frequent as the requests for the remission of a sentence or for restitution. In most cases he gave, sometimes he lent, and then the loan appeared on the accounts of the *Intendant-Général*. It was a mere question of account, for the creditor never reclaimed the debts. Most frequently, on the occasion of a baptism or a marriage, he put the note at the bottom of a basket, covered it with some jewel or sweetmeat, and sent it to the debtor. Some, however, he did not lose sight of, and had kept on the accounts up to 1815.

If the sum granted was important he scrawled an order on the Treasury; if smaller, he took a rouleau from his drawer, or, calling his secretary, had it paid out of the petty cash. He did not like to be thanked, and would not allow it even from those most familiar with him, those whom it was his pleasure to load with kindnesses without the trouble of asking for anything. He either sent them away with the gratuity, or he slipped into their hand a scrap of paper, and on that paper a figure—a big figure—of money, to be drawn from Estève.

There was never any familiarity,—he kept to his rank; to show that the audience was finished, in most cases a sign of the head, sometimes a glance at the list on the table, sufficed. He never gave his hand. A century ago shaking hands was a mark of equality, and was scarcely ever used by a superior to an inferior; and as to kissing hands, which the Bourbons re-established, Napoleon thought it a little degrading. There were, therefore, none of those external marks so freely used later, which became so commonplace. On a single occasion, it seems, his feelings carried him away. It was in 1815, at the beginning of the Hundred Days. When M. Molé entered his *salon*—that Molé for whom he proved his confidence and personal esteem by appointing him, at twenty-nine years of age, Councillor of State and Director-General of Bridges and Roads, at thirty-three years Grand Judge and Minister of Justice, reserving for him the succession to Cambacérès, Arch-Chancellor and

Grand Dignitary—on that day then he went up to Molé, pressed his hand and embraced him. It is, we may believe, one of the few cases where, in one of his own palaces, he thus put aside his Imperial dignity. "Otherwise," as he said, "he would have been clapped on the shoulder every day."

V.

DÉJEUNER.

AT half-past nine the *lever* and the audiences should have come to an end, for it is the hour fixed for *déjeuner*, but most frequently the audiences lasted till eleven o'clock, the *Préfet* of the palace is waiting, and the *déjeuner* gets cold. No precaution is taken against poison; the regulation indeed says that dishes from the kitchen and of confectionery are to be brought in covered, as well as the water, the bread, and the wine, and that as soon as the table is laid out a *maître d'hôtel* was always to remain in charge; but as the table, a very small round table of mahogany, cannot be placed in the *salon* in which the Emperor is giving audience, the *déjeuner*, on silver plates, with covers surmounted with an eagle, and placed on dishwarmers filled with hot water, which is renewed as required, goes on simmering in a corner of the ante-chamber until the Emperor gives notice that he wishes to eat. The small table is then quickly arranged and covered with a napkin by the carver; the *Préfet* of the palace, in a fine coat of amaranth embroidered with silver, walks before the Emperor, and stands near to the table, the service of which is performed by the *maître d'hôtel* of the Emperor, Guignet, known as Dunan.

This Guignet is of a family all of whom have been employed in the service of the king and of the princes of the house of Bourbon. Another Guignet was still *valet-de-chambre* to Louis XVIII; a female Guignet was in charge of the linen of Marie Antoinette. Guignet, called Dunan, was himself the son of a cook of the Prince de Condé, and having served his apprenticeship at the Palais Bourbon, became *chef* to the Duc de Bourbon when on his travels, followed him into emigration and was then his cook. Wearied out with the travels of the army of Condé, he found a place with the Prince Louis de Rohan, then succeeded in re-entering Paris, and was favourably received in the household of the First Consul, in which he became *maître d'hôtel* after Lecler obtained the place of custodian at Versailles. Dunan had a yearly salary of 6,000 francs, besides frequent gratuities, the largest in 1810 of 3,000 francs. In this royalist origin he was not exceptional. Most of the principal servants, the ushers, and the grooms were brought up as he had been, and it is curious to find the same names among the servants of the Pretender at Hartwell, and among those of the Emperor at the Tuileries.

The *maître d'hôtel*, in a green coat embroidered with silver (a coat which cost 500 francs), with a white waistcoat, black knee-breeches, white silk stockings, and shoes with buckles, presented his *menu* the evening before to the first controlling *maître d'hôtel*, who discussed it in the office of the Control, submitted it to the *Préfet* of the palace on duty, and gave the orders to the appointed and sworn purveyors. The articles of food were delivered, carefully packed, at the office of the Control by porters who were known there and approved. The articles were weighed, examined, and measured by a sub-controller, then passed on to the *maître d'hôtel*, who personally superintended the execution of his *menu*.

This *menu*, by the Emperor's orders, was very limited, and gave no room for the imagination of Dunan to display itself. In 1810 the *déjeuner* was to consist of one soup, three *entrées*, two *entremets*, two dishes of dessert, a cup of coffee, two rolls of bread, and for drink a bottle of Chambertin. At a later time the *menu* was still further reduced, and consisted of two soups, a roast, one *entremets*, two *hors d'œuvre*, four plates of dessert (compote, fruit, cheese, and sweetmeats), and coffee.

The Emperor allowed these to be put before him, but he never touched so many dishes. He ate very quickly, not over cleanlily, often putting his hand in the dish and making many splashes on his clothes. He followed no particular order, but passed from the *entremets* to the *hors d'œuvre*, and then returned to the roast. He restricted himself to none of the rules usual in a classic repast, and masticated large mouthfuls very imperfectly in his haste to be done. The meal usually lasted no more than seven or eight minutes. What he preferred was fowl, with any kind of sauce, *poulet sauté à la provençale*—without garlic, for garlic disagreed with him—fowl *à l'italienne, à la tartare, à la marengo,* fowl fricasseed, *sauté*, or roasted. He was very fond of fried things and of pastry, *vol-au-vents, bouchées à la reine*, and *petites timbales à la milanaise* ; also of *boudins à la Richelieu, quenelles* of poultry *au consommé*, and above everything of macaroni in the Italian way with Parmesan cheese. Of fish he placed before everything red mullet from the Mediterranean—that was one of his treats. After Egypt, for a long time the usual dishes of his table were pillau and dates, but this was one of the fancies, not of his appetite, but of his imagination ; just as when he used to believe, with great sincerity, that he preferred the soldiers' soup to delicately made soups, and valued above all vegetables, potatoes, haricots, and lentils.

Those who served him did not willingly admit such tastes, for it was the time when the great French *cuisine* still had its traditions, when it was still a point of honour with the *maîtres d'hôtel*, and when the composition of a *menu* was an honour or a dishonour to its author.

So that when the Emperor asked Dunan why he never gave him pork *crépinettes* (a sort of sausage), Dunan replied that it was because they were indigestible, but " really," said he, " because he thought them scarcely consistent with good living, and scarcely of a nature to do honour to the Imperial *cuisine*." The next day he sent up *crépinettes* of partridge, and the Emperor found them excellent, and eat heartily of them. It was in this as with his clothes ; " The pay of a captain is enough for me," he was fond of saying. And in the course of the night, the morning, and the day, he changed his linen and his dress three times in twenty-four hours !

Very fastidious, he would scarcely eat French beans, of which he was very fond, for fear of finding them stringy, which he said had the same effect on him as hairs, and the mere thought of hairs in what he ate turned his stomach. At Cherbourg, however, in May 1811, having taken a fancy to go and breakfast on the mole, he stopped at a guard-house and had some of the ammunition bread and the soldiers' soup brought him ; the first thing he found in the soup was a long hair. In spite of his turning against it he took out the hair and ate the soup. But the soldiers were looking at him.

Of roast meat he looked out for the part which was most done, " the brownest," and he had a horror of underdone meat. The dishes at *déjeuner* were all served up at once, and he took off the covers himself from the dishes, which were at once removed when the contents did not please him. When it pleased him too much, he scolded ; " Monsieur," said he to his *maître d'hôtel,* "you can see plainly that you make me eat too much, and I don't like that. It makes me uncomfortable. I only wish to have two dishes served."

Sometimes he was capricious, which now and then was followed by loss of temper. Dunan, having seen that the *crépinettes* of partridge pleased his master, a month afterwards put them again on the *menu.* The Emperor uncovered the dish, got in a rage, pushed the table away, upset it on the carpet, and retired to his study. The servants hastened to clear away the table service, and Dunan, like a worthy descendant of Vatel, went at once to the Grand Marshal to give his resignation. Duroc consoled him, sent him back again, and told him to prepare a second meal. In fact the Emperor asked for it. Roustam handed the *déjeuner* to the Emperor, who called for his *maître d'hôtel*. Dunan arrived very mortified, and served a roast fowl. Napoleon complimented him on it, gave him a few taps on the cheek, and said, "Ah! Dunan, you are happier as my *maître d'hôtel* than I am as Emperor." He had these ways, which were like excuses, even to a *maître d'hôtel* or a *valet-de-chambre*, after his short outbursts of anger, or rather his fits of impatience, which resulted from causes quite removed from the immediate object which provoked them.

The Emperor scarcely ever drank anything but Chambertin, mixed with a great deal of water. He had no cellar of wine, either at the Tuileries or in any of the palaces. The supply was contracted for by wine merchants named Soupé & Pierrugues, carrying on business at No. 338, Rue St. Honoré, who undertook to furnish the required quantities, not only at Paris and in the Imperial *châteaux*, but also on campaign. One of them, for that purpose, always accompanied headquarters. They delivered the wines and liquors in bottles of a uniform shape, manufactured at Sèvres, and marked with a crowned N. They were only paid for the bottles consumed.

The Chambertin of five or six years old which the Emperor drank, cost, like the Romanée, Clos-Vougeot, Montrarchet of the same date, and the Lafitte of ten or twelve years, six francs a bottle. The Emperor was so accustomed to Chambertin that he had great trouble at St. Helena to habituate himself to claret, so that it was one of the petty sufferings of his captivity. From the time of the Egyptian campaign it was the wine which he drank solely, as he himself testifies. When, after the victory of Elchingen, he went on to sleep at Ober-Falheim, where he found that all his baggage was pillaged, even to his Chambertin, he remarked gaily that up to that time he had not been deprived of it, even in the midst of the sands of Egypt. After all, this indulgence is the only one he was known to have, and it was kept within limits, for he never exceeded the half bottle. No other wine was served at *déjeuner*, and no liqueur after *déjeuner*.

There appeared on the Emperor's table a service of silver plate, chased, and decorated with the Imperial arms. Some of the silver, however, dating from the Consulate, was marked with a B. With the exception of the dish-covers, generally surmounted with an eagle, the silver in common use was very plain, and kept to the ordinary patterns; the salt-cellars, for instance, were shells, or swans, or ornamented with a caduceus, the oil-cruets were in the shape of swans. With the exception of the salt-spoons of silver gilt, everything was of silver. Silver gilt was only used at dinner on Sundays, and on grand occasions, contrary to the practice of the princesses, who were always served on silver gilt.

But there was no lack of plate. From the time of the Egyptian campaign, General Bonaparte had for his own use a service of plate, very light and portable, which afterwards served as a pattern for what was called the hunting service; but he had only a few specimens left, all the General's baggage having been stolen between Frejus and Aix. During the Consulate, he was at first compelled to be satisfied with little, and he was only able to supply himself by degrees. The service supplied by Biennais in the year X did not consist of enough large pieces, and he was obliged at every grand dinner to hire. As to the table service, a set of white and gold porcelain was used, marked with a B in gold, supplied by Séjournant, and costing, including cups and saucers with garlands of laurel, carafes, and glasses richly cut, marked with a B, 23,463 francs 30 centimes. Little by little it increased, and in the year XIII, besides the splendid service of silver gilt presented on the occasion of the coronation by the city of Paris, the Emperor possessed a service of silver gilt for twenty-four covers; a new set of silver all marked with the letter B, with ninety-six dishes for *entremets*, ninety-six *entrée* dishes, thirty-two dishes for roast meats, and the rest in proportion; but for dessert as yet he only had the forks and spoons and accessories of silver gilt. As a centre-piece it was necessary to borrow from the *Garde meuble* an Apollo driving the four horses of the sun, which on occasions was accompanied by various statuettes of Hercules performing his labours. In 1806, the silver plate, increased by a series of purchases, reached to the weight of 24,449 hectogrammes. Completed definitely in 1811, it was reckoned, in the palaces of France only, at a value of 2,193,301 francs 48 centimes, without counting 843,791 francs 74 centimes in Tuscany, in Rome, and in Holland.

Napoleon always took his *déjeuner* alone, except during the very short time between his second marriage and the confinement of the Empress. Joséphine never took *déjeuner* with him, and after the birth of the King of Rome the Emperor resumed his solitary habits, which suited him better. From the birth of his son, the *gouvernante* of the children of France, Mme. de Montesquiou, was ordered to bring the child every day at the time of *déjeuner*. He took him on his knees, made him taste his reddened water, and put to his lips a little of any gravy or sauce which came to hand. Mme. de Montesquiou remonstrated, the Emperor burst out laughing—it was for his son, and with his son, that he had his only noisy gaiety—and the infant king laughed with him. The Empress was often present, and was amused also at these little scenes.

Such scenes were familiar to the Emperor, who for a long time past liked to have his nephews brought to him at his *déjeuner*. The picture by Ducis is well known, in which he is represented as surrounded with all the children of the family, who play around him while he breakfasts. It is really at Saint-Cloud; but when, on February 27th, 1809, Baron Lejeune arrived from Spain bearing the news of the taking of Saragossa, and was received at the Tuileries, he found the Emperor seated near a small table, having on his knees a pretty child of three years old. Both of them were taking their meal from the same fork, and during the conversation the Emperor kept caressing the child, the eldest son of King Louis. After his meal the Emperor took coffee. The child, who had stretched out his little arms to take the cup and drink also, was surprised at the bitterness of the liquid, and made a grimace and pushed away the cup. The Emperor laughed heartily, and said to his nephew, "Ah! your education is not complete yet, for you don't know how to dissimulate."

Sometimes, when teased, the child resisted. One day, when he had the two sons of Louis to *déjeuner*, he made the eldest turn his head away, and then took away his boiled egg. The boy, who was three years old, took up his knife and said to the Emperor, "Give me back my egg, or I will kill you!" "What, you rascal! you want to kill your uncle?" The child did not give up. "Give me back my egg, or I will kill you!" And the Emperor gave back the egg, saying to his nephew, "You will be a famous fellow."

With the brother of Napoleon Louis, who died, Napoleon Charles, he had games of quite a different sort. He took him in his arms, showed him the garden, and said, "Whose garden is that?" "My uncle's." He pulled his ears, and said, "When I am gone it will be yours. I hope you will have a good inheritance." He let him do just as he liked, delighted to hear him cry out when he saw soldiers in the garden, "Vive Nonon the soldier!" amusing himself with the fables which he made him recite, playing with him to the extent of holding him on his knee and giving him lentils to eat one by one, having the same weakness for him as in 1804, when he had him brought to Malmaison during dinner, put him on the table, and laughed like a madman to see him help himself from the dishes and upset everything around him.

With the children of Caroline and Elisa these pleasantries succeeded less. Less accustomed to his ways, less respectful towards their uncle, less brought up to love him, and surrounded by more servile attendants, they sometimes got angry, as little Achille Murat, whose ears he pulled, and who rushed at him with clenched fist, crying out, "You are a naughty, wicked man!"

Other children—little Léon, the little Walewski—were sometimes brought to him at *déjeuner*. With these also he was connected, and it was natural that he should put himself out for them; but the children of his servants, like the son of Roustam, whom he caressed, from whom he provoked retorts and the familiar "*tutoiement*," and whose ears he gaily rubbed, could only have amused him because he had a love of children to a remarkable degree. He possessed it so strongly, in fact, that in his laws he put their interests in the very foremost place; and if he had the power of refusing very little to women, there is no example, so to speak, that when a child was employed to ask him a favour, he repulsed him.

It was not children only who were admitted

to Napoleon's *déjeuner*; it was the time when he received artists and savants. Talma was one of the familiar visitors, and the Emperor talked with him about dramatic art, and was pleased to give him advice, advice which was well paid for; for from 1806 to 1813 Talma received from the treasury of the theatres as gratuities, in excess of his regular salary, the sum of 195,200 francs. Another was Denon, the Director-General of Museums, to whom Napoleon discoursed about the pictures which he wished to see executed, of the taste for art which he desired to develop in the nation, and who fulfilled in so distinguished a manner the duties formerly assigned to the Director-General of Royal Buildings.

At first—that is to say, at the time of the expedition to Egypt—when Denon, presented to Madame Bonaparte by Madame de Cresny, his mistress, begged to accompany the General, Bonaparte had a strong repugnance to him. In the first place he mistrusted this Madame de Cresny, who was very intimate with Joséphine, rendered her little services of a very doubtful character, and received from her more substantial services; then he had no fancy for womanly men, who took women to protect them. Thus the Chevalier de Non, at the time when he was Gentleman-in-Ordinary and Secretary of the Embassy, had done nothing else but push himself forward by means of women. What is known about him is not his cautious and patriotic diplomacy which was the cause of his disgrace at Naples. It was his pretty little story, "*Point de Lendemain*"; his amours with Queen Maria Carolina; his obscenities, which with such ability and such freedom he scribbled at every corner; his satyr's head, which, in spite of its ugliness, had never met with cruelty from a woman. It was necessary, therefore, for all the world to busy itself to induce the General-in-Chief to take such a person with him. But soon, during the voyage, and afterwards, while in Egypt, he was delighted with his lively conversation, so able and so full of information; with that indefatigable curiosity which impelled Denon to risk his life to obtain a sketch; with that keen sight, so true and so graphic for contemporary facts; with that encyclopædic information which made him one of the best judges of art, the most competent man to carry through an immense enterprise—that of substituting for the subjects of antiquity or of pure imagination, which artists insisted on treating, subjects taken from the history of their own time. In these conversations of the Emperor with Denon were laid down with precision the subjects of the paintings and the statues which the Emperor caused to be executed. To collect the materials, Denon, accompanied by skilful painters, followed headquarters on campaign, and caused to be drawn under his own eyes, or drew himself, the most interesting scenes. He also went through the museums of conquered towns, and chose the pictures which completed the Musée Napoleon. He afterwards went, furnished with full powers, to Italy, and brought back unique works of art, or made propositions for the purchase of the most important collections. Nothing escaped him, and, owing to him, nothing escaped the Emperor, whose enthusiasm from that time was kindled. He never lost the scent, but followed up the pursuit with an ardour which is astonishing. It is neither the fault of Napoleon nor the fault of Denon that we do not see at the Louvre, near the Borghese statues, by the side of the Aldobrandine Nuptials, the complete series of the Ægina marbles.

Fontaine the architect—in whose honesty and straightforwardness Napoleon had entire confidence, the only man since Mansard who had succeeded in being grand, even in a small space, the only one who in a new style had discovered a method of interior decoration at once severe and majestic—brought his plans for the ideal palace, the palace of dreams which the Emperor delighted to think of, to arrange and to build on paper, and in which he tried to unite and combine all the conveniences of his different headquarters—the palaces of all the sovereigns of Europe.

Then came his companions of Egypt, always welcome: Berthollet the chemist, generally short of money, and who never left without carrying some off; the two geometricians, Costaz and Monge, the latter especially, on whom the Emperor had conferred, together with the title of Comte de Peluse, the high dignities of the Senate and the Legion of Honour.

It was at *déjeuner*, too, that sometimes the official painters were admitted to make a sketch from him—for instance, Gérard. David holds the position of first painter, the duties of which he chose to understand as a sort of dictatorship in art, which gives him the right of presenting himself. As for Isabey, if he appears, it is much less in the capacity of painter of miniatures than as a designer, as the inventor of coats of arms, and arranger of the ceremonies; but the favour which he enjoyed at the time of the Consulate has somewhat passed away, and, in consequence of certain familiarities which he indulged in, he lost the altogether exceptional position which he might have taken in the household.

With these men, all possessed of talent, of intellect, and of knowledge, the Emperor loved to let the activity of his mind expatiate on all manner of subjects; and each of those who was admitted to these interviews, and who, like Isabey, Monge, Fontaine, and Talma, have left some written record, bear witness to the grace, the amiability, and the gaiety which Napoleon possessed, the grasp of the subject with which he spoke, and the power with which he stored up even the most trifling facts in his retentive memory.

Often, when he had no one else to exchange a word with, he plied with questions the *Préfet* of the palace, who, erect, with his hat under his arm, stood looking at the *maître d'hôtel* waiting at table. "Where was that bought? How much did that cost?" And when he received an answer, he often said, "It was much cheaper when I was a sub-lieutenant. I will not pay dearer than others."

He was compelled to pay, however, when he had in his kitchens—those stifling kitchens of the Tuileries, in which all seasons were alike, "where no one could decay on account of the coal smoke" (it was Fontaine who said this) —artistes such as Farcy, first *chef*; Lecomte, *chef*; Lebeau, head pastrycook, who was, it is said, "the regenerator of French pastry," and who, on entering the household of the First Consul, made a sensation by the pretty *pièces montées* of which he was the inventor. At his Quintidi dinners (Quintidi was the fifth day of the Republican week of ten days), a passage of the bridge of Lodi, a passage of the Tagliamento, and especially a passage of the bridge of Arcole, of barley-sugar, biscuit, pastry, and nougat had been much admired as the works of an artist. Lebeau made all the pastry, even for the grand balls. Before he came the *pièces montées* only were supplied by Bailly, pastrycook, Rue Vivienne. We are unable to authenticate an anecdote relating to the price of a *vol-au-vent*, bought out of the house, and sent up by Rechaud; who, besides, was not *maître d'hôtel* to Napoleon, but to Joséphine. It would seem to have been singularly imprudent to have dishes from a pastrycook which were intended for the Imperial table, especially dishes requiring pastry-crust; and this explains why Lebeau is one of the few servants in the kitchen who remained from the beginning to the end of the reign.

The cooks changed very frequently. Was this on account of the bad ventilation of the kitchen, or on account of the rigid economy established in the household, which strictly tied them down to wages of 2,400 francs? After Gaillon, who accompanied the General to Egypt, and who was pensioned off with the place of clerk of the kitchen at Fontainebleau; after Danger, who also made the Egyptian expedition, and who had even run the risk of losing his life when on the way back the plate was stolen at six leagues from Aix, in Provence —we find successively, after 1802, Venard de la Borde, Coulon, Farcy, La Guipière—the artist whom Murat attached to his person and who died on the return from Russia—Debray, Lecomte, Heurtin, Lacombe, Lemoigne; Ferdinand was cook at the Island of Elba. A man named Dousseau was *chef de cuisine* during the Hundred Days. As we see, there was a constant change; but it must be added that among these names are comprised, besides those of *chefs de cuisine* properly so called, those of *chefs* of special departments, who, when a campaign began, were dispersed among the different detachments of the household in such a manner that the Emperor found a complete service in almost every place to which he went. It spite of these frequent changes, it was in the old Imperial household that was found, after ten fruitless attempts, a man sufficiently devoted to go to St. Helena. This was Chandelier, *page rôtisseur* in 1813, who passed into the household of Princess Pauline, and who, as soon as the proposition was made, accepted eagerly the mission of devotion which was offered him. He shared with the other servants the cares which the exile required; and his name, thenceforth immortal, is inscribed in the will.

VI.

THE EMPEROR'S STUDY.

IT was very rarely that the Emperor prolonged his *déjeuner*; it was only on the days when, as he said, he felt the necessity of shutting up his study, and of giving his brain a little repose. On most occasions, after he had taken his usual cup of coffee, he returned to his private apartments; but often before setting to work he went down the little staircase and paid a short visit to the Empress. With Joséphine, the visit coincided with the moment when she was having *déjeuner* with the ladies whom she had invited, and this little excitement amused the Emperor for a few moments. With Marie Louise, whose life was much duller, conversation soon came to an end. Napoleon, who sat down on an armchair, allowed himself to drop off to sleep for a few moments. In the case of either of them it was a mere appearance

NIGHT-WORK.

which he made, for business was waiting, and nothing stood in the way of work.

The room which Napoleon made into his study was of moderate size. It was lighted by a single window made in a corner and looking into the garden. The principal piece of furniture, placed in the middle, was a magnificent bureau, loaded with gilt bronze, and supported by two griffins. The lid of the table slid into a groove, so that it could be shut without disarranging the papers. Under the bureau, and screwed to the floor, was a sliding cupboard, into which every time the Emperor went out was placed a portfolio of which he alone had the key. The armchair belonging to the bureau was of antique shape; the back was covered with tapestry of green kerseymere, the folds of which were fastened by silk cords, and the arms finished off with griffins' heads. The Emperor scarcely ever sat down in his chair except to give his signature. He kept habitually at the right of the fireplace, on a small sofa covered with green taffeta, near to which was a stand which received the correspondence of the day. A screen of several leaves kept off the heat of the fire. At the further end of the room, at right angles in the corners, were placed four bookcases, and between the two which occupied the wall at the end was a great regulator clock of the same kind as that furnished in 1808 by Bailly for the study at Compiègne, which cost 4,000 francs.

While he was still First Consul Napoleon had thought of having made, either in this room or in the neighbouring *salon*, a bookcase composed of sixteen divisions, sixty-six feet in length, and capable of holding ten thousand volumes. The catalogue of the books in the private study, recently published, does not seem to amount to so considerable a number; but the books enumerated could not in any case have been contained in the four bookcases which we see represented. There were books also in the back study, books in the cabinet of the keeper of the portfolio, along the side of the bedroom, and books also in the little apartment.

Opposite the fireplace, a long closet with glass doors, breast high, with a marble top, contained boxes for papers, and carried the volumes to be consulted and the documents in use; no doubt also the equestrian statuette of Frederic II., which the Emperor constantly had under his eyes. This statuette was the only work of art which he ever personally desired to have.

In the recess of the window was the table of the private secretary. The room was furnished with a few chairs. At night, to light his bureau, Napoleon used a candlestick with two branches, with a great shade of sheet iron of the ordinary kind.

The study led into the back study, which was furnished with a few chairs covered with green morocco, and a secretaire with cylindrical lid, adorned with ornaments of bronze gilt and veneered with marqueterie of rosewood representing instruments of music. The decoration of this room recalled its former use as a boudoir. All the subjects painted in it alluded to female occupations, over which, from the ceiling, presided the Queen Maria Theresa, under the guise of Minerva. All along the walls ran a dwarf bookcase. It was in this room that the Emperor generally received his Ministers, and that he granted audience before the *lever*, during the day and in the evening. It cannot be too often repeated that a stranger never entered the study.

We ought to have very accurate information on the decoration of this study, of which four pictures at least profess to give the appearance. In many respects those of Gérard, of David, and of Vigneron agree, but that by Garnier, which Meneval says was made from nature, and which is engraved in the work of Landon, baffles one completely. In it we see busts placed in front of bookcases, statues standing at the end of the room, divided by columns into two unequal parts, bas-reliefs, the whole a combination of magnificence appropriate to a study arranged for display, and not to a study for real work. Meneval states that he had seen this picture again at the house of the Comte Le Marois, who came across it by chance and bought it. Now at the sale of the Comte Le Marois there was a portrait of Napoleon by Garnier, exactly of the same general idea as in the picture engraved by Landon, but without any accessories, and showing nothing of the study. Either Meneval had not seen again, in spite of what he says, the portrait bought by M. le Marois, or his memory deceived him; but, in any case, the study which Garnier represented, and which may be seen in the engraving in Landon, is not that of the Tuileries. Such as the study at the Tuileries was under the Empire, such it remained under the Restoration, and all the descriptions which exist of it agree. The furniture, as we have seen, was bare. As to the decoration, it was just as it was in the time of Maria Theresa. In the panels, fortunately three-quarters hidden by the bookcases, were seven landscapes of Francisque Milet, in the style of Poussin, landscapes of a disproportionate height, and very indifferent, which have turned so dark that nothing is to be made out of them. The other paintings, somewhat less dark, were by Nocret; the painting of the chimney-piece, entirely mythological; the subject was Minerva to whom Mercury presented different women who rendered her homage. Minerva was Maria Theresa. On the ceiling Minerva again, crowned by glory and surrounded with the genii of the arts; in the pendentives, between Milet's landscapes, allegorical medallions,—Sweetness, Fidelity, Candour, Faith, Sculpture, and Architecture. One must be as indifferent to surrounding objects as the Emperor to pass one's life in such a sumptuous and depressing abode and not to experience a morbid desire to alter its appearance.

In the topographic study which adjoined there was no luxury; nothing but great tables and pigeon-holes in which the maps were arranged in perfect order. The room was very low, for after he had asked for Argand lamps to light up the range of pigeon-holes, the director of the office had to beg for smoke-consumers to protect the ceiling from the great heat of the lamps.

There were two little rooms besides; one, occupied day and night by the keeper of the portfolio, had pictures by Noel Coypel, and a ceiling by the same painter representing Aurora surrounded by loves; the other, the antechamber, with a cabinet for the servants of the wardrobe, opened with a wicket gate, guarded by an usher of the Cabinet, on to the corridors of the Tuileries, and by another door into the back cabinet. The keeper of the portfolio on duty wore a coat, waistcoat, and knee-breeches of black kerseymere, with thirty-four frogs on the coat; the usher was in the same costume as his colleague of the Apartment of Honour.

Such was the theatre; and such were the actors. The principal companion of Napoleon was the private secretary, called Secretary of the Portfolio in 1806; the post was filled by Bourrienne up to 1802, by Meneval from 1802 to 1813, by Fain from 1813 to 1814. Fain had served his apprenticeship under Meneval, and supplied his place when required after 1806. These three men were the most advanced in the confidence and intimacy of Napoleon. It was not without grief that he parted company with Bourrienne, and up to the end treated him with a gentleness which is surprising.

Meneval, much less acute, much less intelligent than Bourrienne, possibly somewhat simple, but of very exceptional assiduity, of absolute probity, and of well-tried discretion, was the servant who suited him. He possessed the gift of real and constant presence. With a salary of 24,000 francs, the position and appointments of Master of Requests, the title of Baron, and an annual allowance of 30,000 francs, he was a person unknown to the Court, so completely that in 1813 many of the chamberlains did not know him; he passed his whole life between the private apartments, the secret apartment, and the four rooms which he inhabited at the Tuileries, on the dark corridor, by the side of Constant, on the servants' story. For him there was no going to the theatre, no leave of absence, no holidays, no acquaintances—it was the life of a cloister.

Fain, who from the month of February 1806 had the title of *secrétaire archiviste*, was accustomed to this kind of life when he was called on to fill Meneval's place in 1813. His power of mind was superior to that of his colleague, and his books show it. They are at the same time rigorously honest, perfectly truthful, and scrupulously accurate. Fain, who received a pension from the Emperor in August 1808, received 18,000 francs a year on the lists, an allowance of 20,000 francs was attached to his title of Baron, and he received besides gratuities of considerable sums on different occasions (18,000 francs in August 1808, 100,000 francs June 27th, 1813, 50,000 francs in April 1814, etc.). Meneval and Fain, to whom no doubt must be added a clerk of the archives of the name of Bary, at a salary of 6,000 francs a year, actually formed the whole staff of the Cabinet.

Meneval had as servants of the office the keepers of the portfolio, Landoire and Hangel, who, armed with sabres, the pattern of which the Emperor himself had fixed on, accompanied him on campaign, taking duty by turns. They received a salary of 4,800 francs, and numerous gratuities (of 2,000 to 6,000 francs). They too were held in the most intimate and complete confidence, having been in the service ever since the Consulate at least. Fain had a clerk at 1,500 francs, named Ribert, a supernumerary.

In addition to Meneval and Fain, the Emperor from 1806 to 1809 had a secretary to report on petitions named Déchamps, a special *protégé* of the Empress Joséphine and her private secretary; he was by calling a poet, and undertook any of the duties of that walk in life, from the words of *Ossian or the bards*, an opera in five acts, to those of *La Succession*, a comic opera in one act. Napoleon assigned him a salary of 12,000 francs; but he never appears to have required his services.

Much more important, although only occasionally, and not at first, were the Secretaries of the Cabinet. When the Emperor instituted these offices on Vendémiaire 30th, year XIII, it was his intention that the two Secretaries of the Cabinet, both of them Councillors of State, should be the immediate recipients of his views, one on everything which concerned the army and the fleet, the other on everything which belonged to the interior and to finance. He only appointed one of these officers, Clarke, whose intellect he had valued from the time of the first Italian campaign, during which also he had the opportunity of forming an idea of his character.

Clarke was of an ancient Irish family, for a long time attached to the service of France; his great uncle, M. de Lee, had been lieutenant-general and Cordon rouge; his father was a major in Bulkeley's regiment, with a colonel's commission; his uncle, M. Shee, was secretary general of hussars, and a favourite of the Duke of Orléans, who was most active in helping forward his career. The protection of the Duke of Fitz-James had put him in the way of two pensions, one of 300, the other of 200 livres; but the protection of Shee procured him the rank of captain substitute in the regiment of Orléans Dragoons. As for himself, he possessed that which leads on to success even more than ambition—the faculty of conveniently dropping his protectors when they had ceased to be useful. In this way he let slip the Duke of Orléans, Custine, Carnot, and his own wife, " a *citoyenne* above the average," as he boasted, that he had married during the Revolution, who served him as a certificate of *civisme*, and whom he divorced as early as 1795 ; in the same way he dropped everybody and everything. At this moment he was all for Bonaparte or for Napoleon, and to obtain employment he neglected no opportunity, nor any application, at the risk even of seeming importunate. He succeeded in getting this place and this title, with the large salary of 25,000 francs ; but the inconvenience of having to go and look for him when he wanted to dictate to him soon brought the Emperor back to Meneval, and, in the course of the campaign of 1805, in which Clarke had followed him, he appointed him Governor of Vienna; he then entrusted him with different missions ; in 1806 made him Governor of Berlin, and finally Minister of War in 1807.

The two posts of Secretaries of the Cabinet remained vacant up to the month of February 1809. At that time, on the proposition of

M. Maret, one was given to M. Édouard Mounier, auditor of the Council of State since 1806, and son of Mounier of the Constituent Assembly. But, while the salaries were kept at 25,000 francs, the original powers were greatly narrowed. Mounier became the chief of the office of translators attached to the Cabinet. This office, situated on the Carrousel, in one of the houses not yet pulled down, had extended so greatly in 1812 as to employ ten persons (there were eight in 1809), having salaries amounting to 33,100 francs. The extraordinary expenses of translation amounted, beyond this, to 28,800 francs annually.

Mounier was admirably prepared for such a work. Brought up in that curious institution of the Belvedere, which his father founded at Weimar during his emigration, he had a wonderful acquaintance with English, German, and Italian, and knew the greater part of the European languages. Calling to his side his former teacher Duvau, who wrote German like a German, he organised his office in such a manner that the Emperor was kept constantly *au courant* of all that was printed and published throughout Europe. He accompanied head-quarters in the campaigns of 1809, 1812, and 1813. He received in 1809 the decoration of Knight of the Legion of Honour, in 1810 the title of Baron, an allowance of 10,677 francs from the domains of Swedish Pomerania, and the rank of Master of Requests; in 1811 a share in the *Journal de l'Empire*; in 1813 the Gold Eagle of the Legion, the decoration of Commander of the Réunion, and the post of Intendant of the Crown Buildings. This proves that the Emperor appreciated his services. It remains to be ascertained if he was as trustworthy as he was intelligent. The greater part of the translators introduced by him, such as Gourbillon and Duvau, were suspected; he himself was of doubtful fidelity. He had been attached too closely to Napoleon's person for the Restoration not to overwhelm him with favours out of gratitude for former services.

The second place of Secretary of the Cabinet was not occupied till 1810, and then by M. Deponthon, one of the most distinguished Engineer officers, who made his first appearance with the army of Italy, made all the campaigns, and was attached by the Emperor to his service as orderly officer in 1806. Compelled by the regulations to dismiss him from his military household when he conferred on him the rank of *Chef de Bataillon*, Napoleon had none the less kept him at hand, employed him on missions, and thought of this way of keeping near to him a valuable auxiliary who could see and could report.

Thus the two Secretaries of the Cabinet did not work in the Cabinet, Mounier having his office outside the palace, and Deponthon being most frequently travelling. But there remained two elements necessary for the development of Napoleon's ideas—maps and books; the Topographic Office furnished the one, the library provided the other.

The chief of the Topographic Office, whom the Emperor was wont to consult at all hours, was, without contradiction, one of the most eminent men in his department who ever existed. Since the siege of Toulon the Emperor had been acquainted with this Bacler d'Albe, who even before the Revolution showed a special talent as a draughtsman and constructor of plans, and who had just passed seven years in the Alps to study their cartography and to paint the most picturesque spots. Bonaparte appointed him assistant on the staff of the artillery, and as soon as he was appointed commander of the army of Italy he put Bacler d'Albe in charge of his topographic cabinet. He advanced him step by step until he made him in 1813 General of Brigade, after having conferred on him the title of Baron in 1809, with an allowance of 10,000 francs, not to speak of very frequent gratuities.

Bacler d'Albe was not only occupied, both in Paris and on campaign, in constantly registering on the map the movements accomplished by the armies by sticking in it pins of different colours, and by the same method under the direct orders of the Emperor in laying out operations for the future; for Napoleon he was, if one may so speak, the *realiser* of the map. Endowed with a magical facility, he was capable of representing, simply from the map and without the mistake of a line, the panorama of the places where the Emperor reckoned on giving battle. On these hatchings, on these curves, on these points of black or white, he saw, and made others see, existing as in nature, not an abstract country, but, as it were, the living country of future campaigns. He at once invented or rediscovered that method so justly in favour at the present day; he applied genius to it, and as a painter he has left some representations of his times which are among the most interesting to be met with.

Under the orders of Bacler d'Albe were two geographical engineers, but of moderate celebrity, Duvivier and Lameau, who after 1814 resumed their rank of captains in the corps from which they came. In 1813 he had as deputy-chief of the office only a former officer of the staff of the Emperor, Athalin, who afterwards was *aide-de-camp* to the Duke of Orléans, lieutenant-general, and peer of France.

The library had apparently two librarians; but one of them was there only for the honour and the salary—the Emperor never asked for any service from him. He appointed the Abbé Denina of Turin his librarian because Denina had filled this post, or rather, had had this title, under Frederic II. Thought of the King of Prussia took possession of the Emperor's mind. The study which he made of his campaigns since his youth, and which he resumed at St. Helena; the style of dress which he had taken from him; the statuette of Frederic, the only ornament of his study; the veneration in which he held the trophies carried off from Berlin; the visit to his tomb,—all these, even to the choice of Denina as librarian, show his admiration for him whom he called "the tactician *par excellence*."

The other librarian, during the whole of the Consulate and down to September 9th, 1807, was Ripault. Ripault was a man of great worth, who had accompanied Bonaparte into Egypt. It was he who formed the libraries of the Tuileries, of Laeken, of Malmaison, of Saint-Cloud, of Fontainebleau, of Rambouillet, and the little libraries of the study in all the residences. Besides this duty, from the year XI he was charged with the analysis of all journals which were not political; of all books, pamphlets, plays, bills, placards which appeared during the ten years, with a report of literary and religious assemblies, and of any law proceedings which attracted attention. He was the supplier of information to Bonaparte, who wished, by means of his report alone, to know everything that passed in the world of letters and elsewhere.

Ripault, worn out, retired in 1807. His successor, a much better known man, was Barbier, the celebrated bibliographer, who combined with the functions of librarian to the Emperor those of librarian to the Council of State. With Barbier, Napoleon could be easy. There was not a book with which he was not acquainted, and which he could not procure; not a question which he left without answer; not a scheme of forming a library, wherever it might be and for whatever purpose, which he hesitated to undertake. If Napoleon wanted to form his portable libraries, start a library for the Enfants de France, make a collection of the classics of which a few copies only were printed; if he wanted new novels, or ancient works, everything which had appeared on any question, everything which had been printed throughout the world on a particular country, the answer was ready—very precise, very clear, very complete, with an estimate of the cost, if required; with maps, if maps were necessary. And, side by side with the work of the library, Barbier was also fitted for other occupations, especially in all that concerned the University and the Catholic Church, for he had been in orders; and, although he had divested himself of the priesthood at the Revolution, he none the less remained Catholic in his own way, in the way in which France of a former time was Catholic, from the King to the last of the secular clergy. He held that outside the Gallican doctrines, summed up in the four propositions, there could be neither security for the State, nor guarantee for the Church, which would soon be given over, in consequence of ultramontane exaggerations, to the practice of a devotion which was almost idolatry. Against these practices, and those who propagated them, Barbier did not cease to be filled with indignation; and his views on all these points so closely coincided with those of the Emperor that he became an excellent auxiliary to him, one of the most valuable suppliers of arguments whom Napoleon ever came across. Barbier succeeded in giving a special character to this Cabinet, which was at once the most restricted in the number employed and the most complete in the choice of the persons of which it was composed.

Every one in it had his speciality, and Napoleon spared nothing to furnish each with the tools necessary for his department. As to maps, he bought all the collections which were brought under his notice, even plans in relief, as the one of Switzerland by General Pfiffer, which was not to be had without paying a good price; and in the same way he paid liberally for the plans of his old campaigns; for keeping up to date the maps of states to which war might take him; or for such traces as could be found of the successive itineraries which conquerors had followed in invading this or that country. He shrank from no expenditure when the utility of it was proved to him—but no luxury. In the maps which were engraved by his orders—except in the atlas of the campaigns of Italy—there were no more of those fine title-pages in which the designer had full scope, and placed the agreeable and charming side of art side by side with technical work. Thus, the map of the hunting grounds which he had completed and corrected has only a simple and commonplace title. The grand voyages of discovery, such as that of M. Freycinet to southern lands, for example, the publication of which he paid for, have atlases entirely geographical, in which nothing is done to please the taste. The maps which he used himself were mounted on strong and thick linen, enclosed in cardboard cases covered with sheepskin of ordinary character.

The same with books. He had everything bought that appeared, but treated them without respect, simply as working instruments. The bindings, more generally of calf of indifferent quality, are impressed on the sides with the Imperial arms, and with the name of the library to which they belong; but this is done without taste and without elegance. The only well-bound books to be found with his arms are dedication copies, or works which he had bound for presents. In that case, and when it was a question of showing his munificence, he spared nothing.

The books printed by his orders at the Imperial press, the great works intended to be offered to sovereigns or to dignitaries, will bear comparison with the most sumptuous work which the Imperial press has ever produced. Nothing equals the "Iconographie Grecque," or "Romaine," the "Description de l'Égypte," the "Paris" of Baltard, the "Fêtes du Sacre" and "du Mariage" of Percier and Fontaine, especially the grand book of the "Sacre" by Isabey. As to the bindings, we can judge of the magnificence which was employed by the copy of the

"Musée Français," preserved in the department of engravings at the library of the palace at St. Petersburg. Each volume cost 11,000 francs.

It is true that such books are scarcely portable, and it was that quality which the Emperor esteemed most highly in books for his own use, to the point of wishing to have books printed without any margin for his travelling library. There can be no better proof that it was the quality of their contents which he esteemed in books, and not their outward appearance.

Of this he gave many other proofs; he cut the leaves of the pamphlets and novels with which they filled up his carriage on each journey with his finger, and having run through them threw them out of the door. At Paris and in the palaces they went into the fireplace. If a book interested him particularly he covered the margin with notes either in pencil or ink.

But, beyond pamphlets and novels, everything which showed the slightest degree of utility was rigidly and strictly kept. No book was allowed to get lost; the most minute precautions were taken. After having been entered in the catalogue, the book was stamped

"*Cabinet de l'Empereur.*" At St. Helena, in the absence of a stamp, a seal smeared with ink was used.

For classing them in the cases the arrangement was absolute and methodical ; the library to which he was most accustomed, that of Malmaison, served as a type. In all the palaces the books had to be arranged as at Malmaison. The books of one palace did not do duty elsewhere ; if he carried any of them away on campaign he was careful to return them. The books which he carried off from Fontainebleau to the Island of Elba he restored on his return. A volume of the *Histoire de France*, a volume worth fifteen sous, which he borrowed from the library at Vienna in 1809, and which could not be found, tormented him for several days, and he had the entire work bought to replace the missing volume. Any book which he had seen and read never went out of his memory ; if the librarian could not find it at once, Napoleon described the binding minutely, mentioned the colour of the sides and back, pointed out the place where the volume might have been placed, and in which book-case it ought to be found,

With papers it is just the same—no luxury. Since his accession he had renounced those admirable headpieces which Roger had engraved for the Consular letters and decisions, those vignettes which show so delightful a feeling for art in the midst of the most serious matters. Now perfectly plain paper or parchment is used even for *brevets* and letters patent, for decrees and reports. It is only the fancy of the papermakers which insists on the double watermark; on one side the head of the Emperor crowned with laurels, on the other the Imperial eagle. His letter paper is gilt at the edges because that is etiquette; it is thick and strong; but papers with fancy edges, which at that time formed one of the feminine elegancies, were not to be found in his possession.

On the other hand, no one knew so well as he how to sort papers, documents, and statements. Lists were to be all of like dimensions, clothed in uniform bindings, arranged in identical order. The same with estimates. There are portfolios in which all papers are arranged by the Minister, the key of which he alone has; other portfolios travel from the

Ministers to the Tuileries; the Minister has a key, he has another. And it is he who combines and arranges these portfolios.

For foreign armies and fleets he has boxes with compartments in which slide cards inscribed with the regiments and vessels. He himself ordered Berthier to get these boxes (perhaps from details furnished by Mme. Campan, whose father, M. Genet, introduced this system to the department of Foreign Affairs under Louis XVI), and he paid Biennais the sum of 2,000 francs for these boxes out of the petty cash.

On all subjects he has a collection of information of the same order, dictionaries of individuals arranged by classes or by states. One of the Emperor's nephews relates that every day Napoleon received and carried about on his person, written on a very small piece of paper, a statement of that which he called the fortune of France, and also the state of his own fortune,—that fortune which was only one of the reserves of the nation. He had this paper in his pocket and consulted it many times during the day.

It is this machinery, this spirit of order

and method which he brings to bear on everything, that choice of those around him, which alone are capable, not of explaining, but of rendering credible, the amount of work which Napoleon got through, and which is actually ten times more important than one imagines; for he was not content to grasp the whole, he entered into the smallest detail, and for fourteen years it was he who thought for eighty millions of men.

END OF VOL. I.

Printed by Hazell, Watson, & Viney, Ld., London and Aylesbury.

www.ingramcontent.com/pod-product-compliance
Lightning Source LLC
Chambersburg PA
CBHW021351230426
43666CB00006B/487